MEGA LIFE

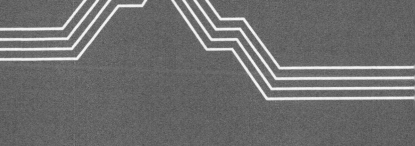

HOW TO LIVE WITHOUT FEAR

Love and Transformation Institute

MEGALIFE
How to Live Without Fear
By Love and Transformation Institute © 2021

Softcover ISBN: 978-1-7339879-4-3
Hardcover ISBN: 978-1-7339879-5-0
eBook ISBN: 978-1-7339879-6-7

Cover Design: Mirko Pohle
Interior Design: Fusion Creative Works, FusionCW.com
Lead Editor: Megan Terry
Book Production: Aloha Publishing

Published by Love and Transformation Institute

Printed in the United States of America

TABLE OF CONTENTS

HOW TO ENGAGE WITH THIS BOOK

Fear holds us back. Many of us are locked in a cycle of anxiety and stress because of fear. *MEGALIFE* is intended to help you live a life without fear. It is an interactive experience where you'll encounter exercises and prompts to help you explore how to live without fear and analyze your own thoughts, beliefs, and actions.

Don't rush through this process. *MEGALIFE* is designed to be completed in eighteen days, although you may need more time with some concepts and responses. Complete it at your own pace.

Our hope is that by interacting with the topics within and taking your time with each exercise, you'll overcome the fear that is holding you back.

Respond to the exercises in the way that's most natural to you. This book is meant to be written in. If you don't like to write in books, keep a journal nearby while you're reading.

We recommend reading *MEGALIFE* with a friend and discussing your thoughts together each day. While you can read *MEGALIFE* alone, you may not get as much out of it without engaging others. If you do end up reading alone, reach out to people around you and ask for their thoughts. Share what you discover.

Welcome to *MEGALIFE*. Get ready to begin living without fear!

"The scariest moment is always just before you start. After that, things can only get better."

—**Stephen King**

DAY
1

What is the most powerful force in the world?

Write your answer here:

_____

Is there anything more powerful than fear?

If so, what is it?

_____

Stop Freaking Out

A mental health crisis is happening in the United States, and even if you don't have a clinical diagnosis, there's a good chance you've been affected in some way. Stress is on the rise, influencing our culture and permeating our lives, especially among young people. Why can't we all just chill out?

According to the American Psychological Association, the majority of Americans are dealing with moderate to high stress, and their stress levels are increasing. The World Health Organization states that one in four people will be affected by a mental or neurological disorder during their lifetime. A survey by *Everyday Health* revealed that by 2019, 52% of Generation Z had already been diagnosed with a mental health disorder.

This is a wake-up call.

Among the many problems our world faces, one of the greatest is our own ability to handle it all. Americans are some of the most stressed people in the world. In the 2019 Global Emotions Report released by Gallup, the United States of America was tied for the fourth most stressed nation in the world alongside Albania, Iran, and Sri Lanka.

Do you feel it? Why is there so much tension?

This tension seems to have created a common goal—we are all looking for answers. You personally might be looking for a way to handle your stress, anxiety, or fear.

There are a lot of methods for dealing with these challenges in life. Have you ever tried exercises or products that are supposed to manage stress?

- Breathe deeply and slowly.

- Meditate once a day.

- Try aromatherapy.

- Get an expensive massage once a month.

These things tend to help by distracting you or helping your body calm down, but when stress triggers reappear, you go back to being a bundle of nerves.

So what are these feelings, exactly, and where do they come from?

Let's try a mental exercise. Wherever you are, take stock of your body. What are you feeling? Is there tension in your shoulders, your stomach, or your head? Are you bouncing your leg?

Now imagine you're lying in bed in the dark, and you've just woken up from a bad dream.

What does it feel like, physically, to have a nightmare?

You wake up with your chest pounding. Maybe you're drenched in sweat. Depending on what kind of nightmare it was, you may be unable to go back to sleep. Maybe you dreamed about something horrific and now you're staring at weird shadows in your room and listening to creaking noises as the house settles.

Or it could have been a dream where you forgot an important deadline, and now there's too much tension in your body to relax enough to sleep again. You feel the urge to get up and go check your email to make sure you didn't actually forget to send in your work.

These two types of anxiety nightmares are associated with different feelings—one fear, and the other stress. But think about the physical feeling you get when you wake up from either one. It's the same: heart pounding, breath short, tightness in your chest, and possibly discomfort in your stomach.

Why do they give your body such a similar reaction? Stress is induced by fear. Sometimes it doesn't feel that way—you're just under pressure to get things done, or you feel uncertain about how circumstances will work out. But what you may not realize is fear and stress are inherently related.

Anxiety and depression are also often linked to fear that surfaces through everyday thoughts and experiences: the fear of not meeting a deadline, being late to work, forgetting to make an important phone call, or making an embarrassing comment. But when something happens that causes this kind of response, it's generally rooted in a deeper fear. You may not recognize it as fear because it doesn't seem like something you should be afraid of. Instead, you feel urgency to take care of the issue or you worry about your inability to handle the problem.

To solve the problem of stress and anxiety in your life, you have to dig deeper and treat it at the root rather than simply addressing the symptoms. While breathing exercises and even medications help calm your body for a time, they don't address the root fear causing the stress to build.

Are you okay?

_____

Where is there tension in your body?

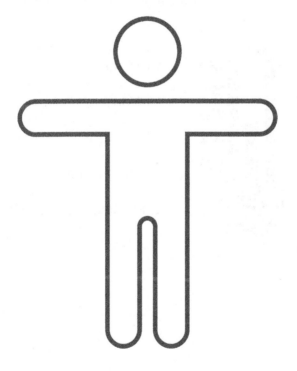

Rate your current stress/anxiety level.

5 (Panicked)

4 (Worried/anxious)

3 (Concerned/mild stress)

2 (Focused/energized)

1 (Relaxed and content)

Dump Your Fear

Stop for a moment and get out your phone. Use the QR code below or type in FearDump.com

We created FearDump.com as a place to leave your fears behind. You can dump as many fears as you'd like. While you're there, take a look at what other people are dumping too. Are there some fears that you share?

It's clear to see that fear is entrenched in our culture and rampant among people of all backgrounds. It deeply affects the way we live our daily lives. We're afraid of things such as whether we'll be able to afford housing, finding and keeping jobs, getting ill, the decisions our political leaders are making, and even failing to live up to our dreams. As a result, many of us lash out at one another, avoid situations that make us uncomfortable, or become overly competitive. Many people believe that living in a constant state of fear is normal.

Though fear is not just an American problem, in the U.S. we are culturally ill-equipped to handle stressful or difficult situations because many of us already live fear-based lifestyles. We make decisions driven by what we *don't* want to happen rather than by what we *do* want.

Fear is a global issue, but it can be stopped! There is a solution to the problem of fear, and we're going to explore it in the pages that follow.

"Of all the liars in the world, sometimes the worst are our own fears."

—Rudyard Kipling

DAY
2

Live Life Outside the What-Ifs

Name a dream you have or something you want to accomplish:

What are you doing to pursue that dream?

Could you be doing more? If so, what's keeping you from doing it?

When a dream or goal goes unpursued, chances are that fear is holding you back. Whether you have a fear of failure or a fear of success, or your inner perfectionist is keeping you in a cycle of procrastination, fear is impacting your life. Think of how much richer your life would be if fear didn't keep you from trying new things, challenging yourself, interacting with new people, or deepening relationships.

It's been said that fear is the greatest motivator. But is that true?

Ancient philosopher Epicurus famously identified the pursuit of pleasure or the avoidance of pain as the two great motivators of mankind. If you're trying to avoid pain, you will be intensely focused on keeping the sources of that pain at arm's length. However, if you're motivated by what you desire to achieve, then your focus shifts from failure and fear to success and hope.

A person might move between different types of motivation throughout their life. When you feel secure, you're more likely to be motivated by things you want rather than things you don't want. But when something undermines that security, we tend to step into defensive mode, and it's hard to experience the pleasures of life because we're so focused on avoiding pain.

This is because fear kills enjoyment.

The messages of fear enter our lives at an early age. From day one, we're told, "Don't touch this; don't do that; don't go there; don't talk to strangers." We are smothered by and overwhelmed with the scary narrative that our world is not a safe place to live.

Lessons of fear were likely driven into us by well-intentioned parents establishing boundaries to help keep us safe. As children, we're taught to fear cars in the street and people we don't know. As we get older, culture and media repeat the same message, but with more detailed descriptions—how horrific a car crash can be, or endless coverage of the most recent tragic event. Of course, it makes sense to be afraid of those things, but if we live in a constant state of fear, everything in our lives is affected.

Living a fear-based lifestyle is living life in the *what-ifs*. There are so many *what-ifs* in our everyday thinking that it's not just about what if something bad happens. What if something good *doesn't* happen? What if I never have a chance to take a family vacation? What if I don't find my soulmate? What if I don't get a promotion? What if I never own a home? We're almost more afraid of lost opportunities and failure than we are of bad things happening.

These *what-ifs* can begin to control your thought life. What if I never get married? What if I never become successful? What if I can't pay my bills? What if one of my children dies? What if I get a horrible disease?

And then there is "FOMO"—the fear of missing out. FOMO struck a chord with so many people that it became a cultural movement. It captured our shared experience by giving language to the common feeling of rapid disappointment through social media exposure. We can all acknowledge that we're afraid of missing out on something good, whether it's simply not attending the party your friends went to or something as large as never having children when you've dreamed of it your whole life.

If you're not careful, fear can take over your life.

What Do You Worry About?

Circle, highlight, underline, or color in the words below that represent things you worry about. If there's something you worry about that isn't on this page, add it.

Being late   Money   Your pet

Debt   Family relationships   Your job

Health   Crime

Friendships   Germs

Your appearance

Romantic relationships

Forgetting to do something important

Natural disasters

The government

Growing old

What other people think about you

Losing something important   Sickness

How many of the worries you selected above influence your behavior? Do you make decisions to avoid the things you worry about? Go back to each one and place a check mark next to it if you can remember a decision you made because of that worry.

Whether or not fear controls your life, you've certainly been influenced by your fears to do or not do things. Believe it or not, there is a concept related to FOMO called FOND—the Fear of Not Doing. Oddly, this kind of fear can make you freeze up and not do anything because you're worried about not meeting your own potential. It results in setting high expectations for yourself and may seem to go away when you focus on completing a task rather than thinking about what you *could* do.

It may be hard to recognize when you're making fear-based decisions because fear is so ingrained that it becomes an extension of your personality.

Don't Let Your Brain Be Hijacked

It's surprising we currently live such fear-driven lives, given that many of the fears previous generations faced are no longer relevant in the modern world. In developed countries we're distanced from many of the things we might truly need to be afraid of, like getting eaten by wild animals or dying of starvation. And most of what we worry about we have no control over. We tend to worry more about what *might* happen than what we are actually experiencing.

Fear is consistently perpetuated by our culture in various ways. Media, especially the news, is one of the biggest players in the game. The media uses fear-inducing stories to sustain their position in the ever-growing *attention economy*—where people are a commodity in their interest of generating revenue. Have you ever found yourself gripped by news coverage because of an event happening in the world? Media has subtle and compelling ways of influencing how you think and feel. Fear is one of the most accessible tools they use for control to keep them in business. In this game, fear is bought and sold.

Examine your thoughts over the last few days. What's been on your mind?

What is happening in your life that consumes a large portion of your mental energy? Conflict in a relationship or at work? A health scare? Politics?

Below, create an estimate of what you spend your time thinking about by drawing lines in the circle to create a pie chart.

Who is hijacking your brain? Who is telling you what you ought to think and feel?

Artificial intelligence (AI) has become so sophisticated that technology giants like Facebook, Amazon, and Google now track every move you make online. They know exactly how ads drive your behavior and how often you need to see them before you will act. You're being influenced more than you realize. Don't think so? Have you seen the Netflix documentary *The Social Dilemma*? It's a must-see, with former executives from tech companies highlighting this exact point. When we let others tell us what to think and feel, those thoughts begin to control our time and energy.

Fear can be forced, manipulated, and used for an agenda. Culture uses fear to tell us how to live for the purpose of consumption. The message might be as simple as, "You need this item or service, and if you don't have it, you're going to be the only one missing out."

Fear is used in politics to win campaigns and to influence opinion.

It can be used by people in positions of power—from school principals to government leaders—to gain control over those they lead.

Your boss might use your fear of unemployment to keep you working overtime.

A parent may use fear of punishment to keep their child from disobeying.

Fear is a tool, and it has been weaponized.

Our brains are also being hijacked by a constant emphasis on the metrics that measure our lives. There's an underlying sense that you have no control over the numbers that define you—your grades, salary, work productivity, credit score, and social media followers. Metrics can be completely unpredictable and yet they often dictate what we can and cannot do in life.

There's nothing meaningful about metrics—they don't inspire us. They also fail to acknowledge the inherent worth and dignity every person has simply by being human. If it's numbers that determine our value, then where do we find meaning in our lives? Numbers are a cold and emotionless means of control.

The well-known episode "Nosedive" from the show *Black Mirror* is a stark example of how ruthless metrics can be. As the scenes play out, each character is judged by an average star rating calculated through their inter-actions with other people. These star ratings deter-mine a person's access and treatment in every part of life. The episode resonates with viewers because it's not far off from where our culture is today. We are under constant pressure to maintain our metrics for fear that they will have a negative impact on our lives.

What happens if you fall behind, are not at your best, or experience an unexpected catastrophe? This sets off an unavoidable chain reaction with consequences that you may never overcome.

You falter in your performance and lose your job.

You forget to study for an exam and your GPA plummets.

You fall behind on your mortgage and lose your home.

The societal pressure to perform and maintain your metrics can be overwhelming. And before you know it, anxiety sets in. Anxiety is the sense that the ground is constantly shifting under your feet. If metrics are all there is to life, then you have reason to be concerned because metrics are always changing, and you can't control them.

Our lives become a game of survival when our value is solely based on metrics and everyone is out to protect their own skin. What is ultimately compromised is our ability to have a deep sense of meaning and worth and therefore the awareness that everything is good with life. And this is exactly where we have found ourselves as our culture sinks ever deeper into a crisis of meaning.

How Does Fear Impact You?

Think about the people in your life—family members, friends, and other people in your social circle whom you know well. Name a few of them.

1.

2.

3.

What are they afraid of?

How does that fear cause them to act?

What would they do if they weren't afraid?

Is someone using their fear as a tool to manipulate them?

What are other ways you see fear affect your community?

"FEAR: False Evidence Appearing Real."

—**Unknown**

DAY
3

The Anatomy of Fear

If we set out to dissect fear, what would we find? What is it made of, and how does it function?

To be clear, the kind of fear we're talking about in this book is not the good kind of fear that creates reverence, respect, or awe. We're talking about toxic fear. The kind that causes a person to constantly be on guard because something unpleasant, dangerous, or painful is always lurking around the next corner.

The classic hit show *Monk* tells the story of Adrian Monk, a former police detective who lives with a laundry list of obsessive fears and phobias. Monk's fears follow him everywhere, accentuated by trauma from his wife's sudden death. As each hilariously awkward episode plays out, we learn that Monk is pretty much afraid of everything: bees, germs, rats, heights, milk, shaking hands, and the list goes on. Monk, in a way, is interesting to us because we can all relate to being afraid of something.

Phobias are common, and they don't tend to require us to dig deep about the reason for our fear. The list of phobias is so extensive that you could literally be diagnosed with a fear of anything.

Have you heard of anatidaephobia—the fear of being watched by a duck?

Pogonophobia is the fear of beards. But that's not as bad as ablutophobia, the fear of bathing. You're really up a creek if you have ergophobia—fear of work. Or maybe it gives you an excuse?

And, of course, there is the worst fear of all—panophobia, which is the fear of everything!

Fears like these are amusing to think about because they seem ridiculous. Phobias are irrational fears. There's no way that beards, bathing, or being watched by a duck can hurt you.

In order to treat these kinds of fears, they must be identified and clinically diagnosed. Diagnosing is part of the clinical method of handling phobias. You must identify them if you want to treat them. And in some cases—such as the fear of work—treating a phobia is incredibly important for the patient to be able to live a normal life.

Clinical or not, we all experience fear. And luckily, there are methods to overcome irrational fears. It is necessary to examine our irrational fears if we hope to get beyond them.

So, what do people fear most today? The list of most common fears, which used to be topped by the fear of public speaking, has changed dramatically. According to research published in *Time*, *USA Today*, and *Inc.* magazines, the top five fears are as follows:

1. Government corruption

2. Identity theft

3. Terrorism

4. Running out of money

5. Losing a loved one

Do any of these fears consume your thoughts? Or have they at times in your life?

If these are the five fears impacting most people, this ought to tell us something about the human experience and about our instincts. It's clear this list is rooted in the relevant problems of our day. While some of these are universal human experiences, such as losing a loved one, others are tied to current events and modern dilemmas.

Every one of these fears poses a threat to the security of what you care about most—your relationships, your livelihood, and your life. And when we dig deeper, we discover they are rooted in foundational fears common to all of humanity.

Recognize the Five Foundational Fears

Psychological studies have revealed five foundational fears that are at the root of all distress.

1. **Failure and rejection.** Sometimes called "ego death," this fear is about damage to your self-image and your social status. We're social creatures, and historically, we needed to stay in groups to survive. Social connection and acceptance are deep emotional needs and are necessary for forming a deep sense of well-being.

2. **The unknown.** Fear of death falls into this category, and it's driven primarily by being unable to know what comes after. But this fear is also expressed in other unknowns—like when we become anxious while anticipating a potential conflict with someone; the suspense that horror movies so readily create; and how the vastness of space, the ocean, or the dark can be unsettling. We don't like what we cannot understand because of the way it makes us feel—unprepared and out of control.

3. **Pain.** We fear experiencing bodily harm. This is closely tied to loss

of autonomy, but it also includes our aversion to experiencing discomfort. This fear serves a purpose in helping keep us out of harm's way.

4. **Isolation.** The fear of betrayal or losing a loved one is part of isolation, which is often at the root of emotional pain. It doesn't have to be complete physical isolation—we can be afraid of being cut off from a person or community we love deeply.

5. **Loss of autonomy.** The loss of autonomy is one of the more complex foundational fears, and it connects significantly to surface-level apprehension. This accounts for the fear of having a lack of control over yourself or your circumstances and the fear of losing your freedom, rights, or privileges.

Now, let's take a look at the chart below to see how each of the top five fears are influenced by a specific foundational fear.

Top Five Fears	Foundational Fears
1. Government corruption	The unknown Loss of autonomy
2. Identity theft	Failure and rejection Loss of autonomy
3. Terrorism	Pain The unknown
4. Running out of money	Failure and rejection Loss of autonomy
5. Losing a loved one	Isolation

You've heard it said that knowledge is power. By understanding how the five foundational fears influence our daily decision-making, you can begin to confront and handle that fear in an appropriate way.

The first step is coming to a greater understanding of your personal fears, and the methods in this book will help you in this process. Sometimes simply acknowledging the reason for a fear can provide relief. But we're going to go further than that. We want to help you change your relationship to fear and learn how you can help others experience the same kind of transformation.

Discover Your Fear Type

It's time to go back to the worries you circled on Day 2. Write down five of them below:

1.

2.

3.

4.

5.

What foundational fear(s) do your worries connect to? Does a theme emerge?

Below are some of the worries you may have circled and the foundational fear(s) associated with them.

Worry	Associated Foundational Fear
Being late	Failure and rejection
Your job	Failure and rejection
Money	Loss of autonomy Failure and rejection
Debt	Loss of autonomy Failure and rejection
Family relationships	Isolation Failure and rejection
Romantic relationships	Isolation Failure and rejection
Friendships	Isolation Failure and rejection
Crime	Pain Loss of autonomy
Your appearance	Failure and rejection

Worry	Associated Foundational Fear
What other people think about you	Isolation Failure and rejection
Growing old	Loss of autonomy Pain Isolation
Your pet	Isolation Pain
Forgetting to do something important	Failure and rejection
Germs	Pain Loss of autonomy
Sickness	Pain Loss of autonomy
Losing something important	Loss of autonomy
Natural disasters	Pain Loss of autonomy The unknown

To get the most out of this book, it's best to determine which of the five foundational fears you want to focus on. Pay close attention to the foundational fear that occurs most often on your list.

This is your fear type. Write it in the box below.

Understanding your fear type will help you see how fear influences your life. It's simply a reflection of the way you often experience fear related to current stressors and your circumstances.

The Root of Fear

As we've already seen, human beings share the same five foundational fears. What's challenging is to determine if fear is hard-wired into us or learned. However, we can be certain that our relationship to fear continues to develop as we experience life.

Trauma is a primary cause that contributes to fear over time. Events that are distressing and disturbing impact the way we think about and respond to life. Many people will encounter enough significant trauma in their lifetime that it dramatically influences their development.

In his book *The Body Keeps the Score,* Bessel A. van der Kolk writes,

"We have learned that trauma is not just an event that took place sometime in the past; it is also the imprint left by that experience on the mind, brain, and body."

The imprint that trauma can create is the reason why post-traumatic stress disorder (PTSD) exists as a clinical diagnosis. Our bodies reveal the results of our fears, and the evidence suggests that it's killing us.

In 2019, CNN's doctor Sanjay Gupta partnered with HBO to release a documentary titled *One Nation Under Stress*. His work was motivated by the fact that middle-aged working-class life expectancy had decreased for two years in a row—something that hasn't happened since the Great Depression. Then, while producing the film, the life expectancy of his targeted people group fell for a third time! Gupta discovered that the culprit was "death by distress." People were dying by suicide, drug overdose, and alcoholism at record rates because of trauma in their life.

While trauma has recently become a trendy buzz word, Gupta's work highlights why it's so important to understand the root of fear—your ability to process fear in a healthy way may literally save your life.

Everyone has trauma in their past, and it doesn't have to be severe to leave you with lingering fear. The purpose of this next exercise is to help you identify your primary fear. Understanding your fear is the first step toward healing and kickstarting the growth process in your life.

What Are You Afraid Of?

Let's go back to your list of fears and worries. This time, choose just one. Name it.

I'm afraid of/worried about _____.

Now it's time to do a mental exercise. Ask yourself the following questions:

1. Is this fear something I've experienced before?

2. What is the base fear it's rooted in?

    a. Failure/rejection

    b. The unknown

    c. Pain

    d. Isolation

    e. Loss of autonomy

3. What formative experiences have I had where I experienced that base fear?

Your fear or worry could come from more than one formative experience. For now, simply identifying what is at the root of your fear will help you better understand it so you can begin to change your relationship with fear.

Fear and Your Brain

Fear serves a purpose. You *should* be afraid.

Emotions are signals to your brain that help you interact with your environment. The emotion of fear functions like an alarm. Generated by the limbic system in your brain, it's designed to trip when you interpret something as a threat. It sends a warning signal, motivating you to react so you can avoid danger. It gets your attention and drives you to action.

You probably live in an environment where you're rarely, if ever, in immediate danger. However, you've probably experienced a time when you perceived something as a threat that actually wasn't. In that moment, hyperarousal set in like a flash in the form of an adrenaline rush. Just like a car alarm, your fear alarm can go off for no good reason. That doesn't mean you should ignore it—instead, run the threat through your rational filters to verify that it's truly a false alarm. Is the fear useful? Is it telling the truth?

We must recognize when fears are useful because they enable us to take necessary action. Just like a healthy amount of anxiety can help you get something done in a timely manner, fear can be healthy when it helps us to take the appropriate action in a given situation. Fear is what keeps us from touching a hot stove or from running a red light.

But fear becomes unhealthy when it doesn't serve a purpose and begins to invade your life.

To create a better relationship with fear, you will first need to learn to filter the emotional responses you have when fear is triggered. This is important because handling your emotional response appropriately is what will inspire you to take action.

The problem is that the instinctual reaction you have in response to fear is not always the best action to take. When your alarm goes off, your body goes into fight-or-flight mode. Your body has one of four responses in a state of panic: fight, flight, freeze, or fold.

For example, if you come across a bear while hiking, you have good reason to be afraid. Thus, your alarm system trips and you feel fear. Then you react in one of the four following ways.

1. **Flight.** You run from the bear. The bear can run faster than you, so this may not be the best choice.

2. **Fight.** You attack the bear. The bear is bigger than you and has claws and sharp teeth, so this could also be a bad course of action.

3. **Freeze.** You panic and freeze in place, paralyzed by fear. This keeps you from assessing the situation and taking any action, making you an easy meal.

4. **Fold.** You panic, collapse, and pass out. You've now become an easy target for the bear.

The best solution in this scenario may be dependent on your circumstances. Perhaps you have bear spray or a gun on you, but if you give in to your instincts before assessing the situation, you may not remember that you're armed. (If you don't have these things, the best advice is to stand and face the bear directly. If you're attacked, lay flat on your stomach with your hands on your neck to protect your vital organs and brain stem.)

The same holds true in a fear-triggering circumstance when you're not in immediate danger. If you allow your fear to keep you from thinking clearly and acting appropriately, you may end up in worse circumstances.

Say you end up in a minor car accident. Your immediate response may be panic. You don't stop to assess the situation and allow fight-or-flight mode to take over.

If you choose flight, you flee the scene and may later be caught and charged with a hit-and-run. If you choose to fight and argue with the other party, they may be angry and try to retaliate. If you freeze, you may not get the insurance information you need, and if you fold, you may admit guilt when it was not truly your fault.

The best course of action is to remain calm, as you're not in immediate danger. This allows you to take the proper steps to report the accident.

You can't live *completely* free of fear because you can't stop your limbic system from firing to give you a warning. It's subconscious. When your limbic system is triggered, adrenaline kicks in, and that adrenaline can be useful. You may have heard stories of people lifting cars to get babies out from under them because of the motivating physiological aspect of fear.

Fear is certainly useful, but it only works properly when you have a healthy relationship with it.

Is your relationship with fear motivating or paralyzing?

What level of fear are you living with? A healthy relationship with fear motivates you to do the things you need without impairing your life or paralyzing you.

Negative fear interferes with your ability to learn and enjoy life. You can't operate properly when your stress levels increase because of fear.

On the other hand, healthy fear can make you smarter by telling you to watch out, but it crosses over to unhealthy fear when it is no longer a tool for motivation and instead becomes a fixation.

You can understand the level of fear you have by examining what you're preoccupied with. What's dominant on your mind all day? It could be something small like paying your bills or something large like a pandemic.

What does your mind wander to when you're driving alone or while in the shower? If you find you can't focus on positive things or don't have time to daydream because you're too busy worrying, then you're living with an unhealthy level of anxiety.

What's the first thing you think about in the morning? What keeps you up at night? What makes you tune out the radio when you're driving? What's the monster hiding in your closet?

A healthy level of fear allows you to acknowledge that yes, you do need to pay the bills, but if you're preoccupied with worry about the bills to a point where you feel that your life will fall apart if you pay a bill late, you become controlled by that worry and fixated on it.

A healthy fear is being wary of strangers, because you don't know their motivations, but if you're so distrustful of strangers that you have anxiety every time you're in public, that's a problem.

We want you to understand your relationship to fear so you might not be so scared of fear itself. A right relationship to fear acknowledges that the good kind of fear is your friend, not your foe. However, fear becomes your foe when it paralyzes you or when you fixate on it.

We ultimately have to make a choice about how much we'll let fear control our actions.

Fear is the greatest thing that holds us back from meaningful success, healthy living, deep relationships, pursuing our dreams, and taking risks. But fear itself is not the problem. It's our relationship to it.

Reframe Your View of Fear

1. We all have it.

2. It's not all bad. It can help us.

3. It becomes negative when it enslaves us.

What Is Your Relationship With Fear?

Go back to your list of fears one more time. Write down the top five again:

1.

2.

3.

4.

5.

For each of the fears above, write "rational" or "irrational" next to it.

Then, ask yourself the following questions about each:

1. How does this fear manifest in my life?

2. Is this fear useful? Does it cause me to take needed action, or does it keep me from doing what I need to do?

How many of your fears enslave you? How many are healthy versus unhealthy fears?

Choose one fear you'd like to change your relationship with, then focus on that for the following chapter.

Which fear would you like to start with?

_____

"Too many of us are not living our dreams because we are living our fears."

—**Les Brown**

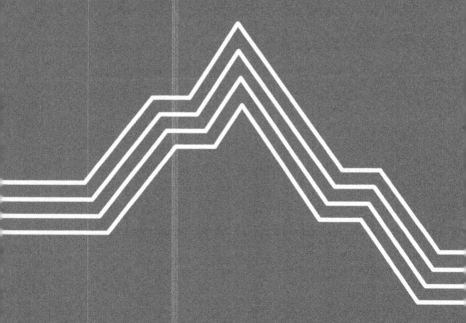

DAY

4

How We Experience Fear

Handling unhealthy levels of fear and anxiety isn't as easy as simply making a choice. When these patterns are pervasive in your daily life, you have to learn how to interact with fear before you can make progress. This journey will take time, but it starts by addressing your individual worries in practical ways.

Neurological research has revealed that our brains interpret the world emotionally before they process it logically.

Does this fact surprise you?

Every experience you have runs through your body and up your spine, entering the emotional center of your brain (amygdala) before it finds its way to the place of logic (prefrontal cortex). So if you want to change our relationship to fear, you must learn how to address it in the order you experience it: emotionally, physically, then logically. While this might seem counterintuitive, developing this skill will dramatically change the way you handle fear.

Let's begin by taking a look at the three levels of fear.

1. The **emotional** level is where you first encounter fear. It's at this level where you experience the sensation of alarm signals getting triggered in your brain. If the fear is pervasive, you will certainly notice a decrease in your overall sense of well-being indicated by increased bodily response.

2. The **physical** level of fear is where bodily responses to fear are exposed: your hyper-vigilant state, pounding heartbeat, sweaty palms, tension headache, or even all-out panic. This is where fear can destroy your life by paralyzing you if you don't have a strategy for maintaining calm. If your relationship to fear is healthy, this is the level where it should motivate you to take appropriate action.

3. The **logical** level is where what you think either helps you act or exacerbates the fear. These thoughts may be rational or irrational and can influence the emotional and physical levels. If the trigger is seeing a bear in the woods, you might think something along the lines of "That bear is going to attack me." If the trigger is running late to work, you might think, "My boss is going to

fire me." However, these thoughts may not be rational. Proper thinking is critical at this level to mitigate fear because the logical level is where you decide to act.

So, you must learn to confront fear in a healthy way on each of these three levels. When you do, your relationship to fear begins to change. Following are descriptions of how to interact with fear emotionally, physically, and logically to begin experiencing progress.

Emotional: Name It

The emotional aspect of fear is the most difficult level to control because you can't turn off your internal alarm system. But there are ways of improving your emotional response to a fear or worry.

Start by thinking about what the fear does to your life before you experience it. How do you feel? How afraid are you? How much does this fear control you?

You can do this in writing or in your head, but it's best to talk about it with someone else. Give it a name. Admit to it, and then process it.

Confronting fears on an emotional level in a healthier way happens by thinking through them in advance. Bring them out into the open. If you find this challenging, you may need to seek professional help with this step. But simply being open about a fear and receiving validation from others can help, especially if you choose people who will not dismiss the fear but acknowledge it and support you.

Create the emotional space in your life to deal with the fear. Emotions don't just go away. Instead, you have to learn to manage them. And you can't do it alone. You need the support of others to make this possible.

Finally, go back to the logical step to support the emotional step. Tell yourself the truth about your fear and believe it. You may have to continue to repeat the truth until it becomes ingrained—that the outcome you dread is unlikely, that it's impossible for your irrational fear to hurt you, or that the situation is out of your control and therefore not worth worrying about.

Logical: Rationalize It

In the process of experiencing fear, you will eventually approach the moment where you need to use logic. And this is a critical point because it's easier to control your thoughts than your emotions.

Your alarm bells have gone off. Now it's time to decide whether the concern is legitimate. Ask yourself the following:

1. Is the concern realistic? How at risk are you?

This is where you determine whether your fear is rational or irrational. Irrational fears are things that won't hurt you, but you likely can't change the way you feel by rationalizing the fear.

2. What are the chances of the negative outcome occurring?

If the fear is rational, how likely is it to occur? The truth, of course, is that the majority of things people worry about never come to pass.

3. Is it preventable? What can you do to mitigate the chances? Or is it out of your control?

Whether or not the outcome is likely, there may be things you can do to lower the chances of it occurring. If it's something you *can* control, take action. Let the fear motivate you to improve your situation. If there is nothing you can do and it is out of your control, you must acknowledge and accept that. We often are less afraid of the inevitable. Acknowledging that something is outside of your control allows you to surrender responsibility for it, removing the feeling of urgency that comes with confronting fear.

Physical: Confront It

To handle the physical aspect of fear, you must understand what's happening to your body so you can respond appropriately. The best reaction is more about knowing what *not* to do. Your fear reactions are fight, flight, freeze, or fold. In most situations, you'll want to avoid those reactions. If you can recognize when you're giving in to your instinct to react in one of these ways, you can take action to respond more appropriately. Whatever you do, don't over- or under-react, and don't tune out or withdraw.

Resist your natural reactions by staying engaged, persevering, and being willing to struggle to reach a better outcome. First, assess the situation before you take action. Make a plan. You need to take the time to process through your fear on both emotional and logical levels so you can plan your actions. Even if you feel terrified while doing this, if you stop and address the fear both emotionally and logically first, it will help you gain a sense of control over the situation.

Adventurer and mountaineer Brian Dickinson is not unfamiliar with situations that generate fear. He has stood on the highest peak in each of the seven continents and is one of only two men to have summited Mt. Everest solo! The book *Blind Descent* chronicles his courageous climb in 2011. Alongside his guide, Brian made it to the third and highest camp on Everest. However, on the day they set out to reach the summit, Brian's guide became so sick from the altitude he had to turn around and head back to camp. The conditions were good, so Brian decided to continue alone. When he reached the top, he had just enough time to look around and take a selfie at the highest point in the world before he went snow-blind. Now Brian was facing one of the greatest challenges of his life. He had to traverse Everest with no eyesight. A descent that should have taken him three hours ended up taking seven. If it wasn't for the guide ropes along the entire route, he would have been dead.

Brian survived because he was able to keep a calm head and not let his fear overtake him. He didn't allow his fight, flight, freeze, or fold reaction to kick in. Instead, he rationalized and walked through the obstacles, eventually making it to safety. The experience was treacherous and undoubtedly terrifying, but Brian made the decision to stay engaged and struggle through the challenge. In Brian's own words about dealing with fear, "If you panic—you're dead!"

By giving yourself the time to process the fear emotionally before you're in a situation where you must confront it, you become more prepared to handle the experience. When you're truly terrified of something, even that emotional processing can be frightening. But you must do it while you're in a safe space and develop a plan for what you'll do when you have to confront your fear.

You can apply the strategy to any situation that makes you uncomfortable or anxious. For example, it's natural to process through a hard conversation you know you're going to have ahead of time. What are your options? What are the directions this situation could go?

And how would you respond? When you anticipate something and you're already prepared for a variety of outcomes, the actual outcome usually ends up not being as bad as you thought.

Sometimes the only way to really confront a fear on a physical level is to actually walk through it. When you go through the experience you're dreading, especially in the case of irrational fears, you may find out it's not so bad. There's a struggle on a physical level where you have to experience the fear so your body comes to understand that you can survive, that you're resilient, and that whatever you thought was going to hurt you may actually be harmless.

Whatever fear you're facing may feel like Everest, but you can make it through. Confronting it on a physical level is often the most difficult step, but it is also the most important.

Changing Your Relationship to Fear

Name it, rationalize it, and confront it—these steps give you a coping method that brings you closer to overcoming your fear by processing it. It's a metabolization process where you work through an issue and allow yourself to absorb whatever is healthy and expel whatever is not, just like our bodies do when we eat.

We know we have fears for a reason, and some fears are useful. But even for those that are the result of trauma, there are things we can gain from metabolizing our fears. We learn lessons and gain skills through processing fears—things that allow our character to grow, like perseverance and patience, empathy and awareness, trust and confidence. Yes, these things may come at a price, but we often grow the most in our struggles. We learn more about ourselves and are better prepared for whatever may happen in the future.

Along with learning from our fears, processing them allows us to recognize what is unhealthy about them and what is not useful. It can be harder to let go of the bad than to learn from the good, and it may take time. But there is more to this process. Metabolizing gives you a healthy way to process your fears on an emotional, physical, and logical level. But ultimately you need to change your relationship to fear to become a less fearful person. That doesn't mean you'll never be afraid again, but it does mean that you can live your life unhindered by fear.

Your emotions are not reliable. They don't discriminate based on what is *worth* fearing. Emotions are only signals—like a check engine light, they only tell you that something is wrong, not what the problem is. Sometimes there is no real problem, and it's just a malfunctioning sensor. If you trust your emotions, you will be afraid of all kinds of things that are not worth fearing.

Can fear be defeated? Is it a choice? People do say *no* to fear. You can choose whether or not to fixate.

Historical figures have shown us that you can stand up and say, "No, I will not be afraid." Freedom comes to those who do. Think of Rosa Parks. She had very good reason to be fearful when she resisted cultural pressure, and she said no.

Maybe you're afraid of being afraid. Maybe you're afraid that people are manipulating you. If so, you don't have to yield to that. You don't have to be a slave to it. It is possible to change your relationship to fear so it no longer controls you.

Your Life Without Fear

In the space below, envision what your life would look like without fear. Draw a picture, make a list, or write whatever comes to your mind.

"There are two basic motivating forces: fear and love. When we are afraid, we pull back from life. When we are in love, we open to all that life has to offer with passion, excitement, and acceptance."

—**John Lennon**

DAY
5

The Opposite of Fear

World renowned scientist Marie Curie has been affectionately referred to as the "Mother of Radioactivity." One of only two females to have won a Nobel Prize in Physics, her life's work studying radiation formed the foundation for cancer diagnosis and treatment. Marie was a brilliant scientist who changed the world with her discoveries, but it may be her observation about fear that's her greatest legacy.

*"Nothing in life is to be **feared**, it is only to be understood. Now is the time to understand more, so that we may **fear** less."*

Often the way to understand something clearly is by learning about what opposes it.

So, what is the opposite of fear?

Dictionary.com lists 21 words as antonyms for fear. Some of those words include assurance, calmness, confidence, contentment, encouragement, faith, happiness, joy, and trust. The last word on the list, which is not referenced here, may cause you to pause: A word that would not naturally come to mind when you think about the opposite of fear. A word that we are so familiar with today that it may have caused us to become unfamiliar with its actual power.

You might think it's courage, but it's not.

While courage is helpful for confronting fear, it's actually not the opposite of fear. The opposite of fear must be equal to or even more powerful than fear itself. It must be able to meet and even beat fear at its own game. It also has to be good and just and worthwhile. This is why courage cannot be its opposite. People can do courageous things, but they can be done with evil intentions. Consider the countless soldiers in history who've survived battle by confronting fear while defending an evil agenda. Did they have courage? The answer is yes. Is it possible to exercise courage for a cause but do it for the wrong reasons? Yes, and that is why courage is not fear's opposite.

So, what is the opposite of fear?

Love.

Wait a minute—isn't the opposite of love hatred?

Not exactly. The opposite of love is control. And there is no greater way to exercise control than to incite fear. Let's look again at the response of the brain to fear: fight, flight, freeze, or fold. When fear enters our brains, it controls our behavior. And fear does not discriminate. It treats everyone the same—with indifference.

There is no more tangible example of this than the events of 2020. A year that began with so much hope and promise quickly spiraled out of control, or should we say, into control through fear. Many people were overcome with the fear of getting sick and dying from the global pandemic. For others, it became about trying to survive. Then there were those who became fearful because of how brutal humans can be to one another or the fear that the lockdown situation would never change. There was fear that came from those fighting for their rights in the wrong way, and fear about what would happen on election day. Fear that if one man won there would be more of the same and fear that the other man would bring too much change. Fear of being ostracized for something you say and fear that our culture may never return to normal.

In the midst of it all stands love, which is the constant appeal that people make: "If there was just more love, then everything would be okay."

But when we say "love," what do we actually mean?

Have you noticed there is global conversation about love taking place? It has been happening for some time now and shows no signs of slowing down. You have seen it and been encouraged to participate. We're told it's the solution to everything.

Something quite peculiar happens when people of influence are asked what will solve the hatred and divisiveness that plagues humanity—the answer is almost always love. A perfect example of this took place during the Super Bowl halftime show in 2016. As Coldplay's front man Chris Martin was concluding the song "Up and Up" alongside Bruno Mars and Beyoncé, he added the lyric "believe in love." At that moment a wave of colored cards filled the stadium spelling out the phrase in huge letters for all the world to see. The appeal these global superstars made to us is to a common sentiment about love we all supposedly share.

If we would just love each other more, everything would be fine. Racism would cease, acceptance would prevail, and harmony would ensue. In a sense, they're right. But to truly do this we have to be willing to give something up. We have to be willing to acknowledge that maybe we don't know as much about love as we think we do.

At the Love and Transformation Institute, we believe that society is not as divided as it appears. Instead, we believe we've never been more united than we are right now.

We're united around one desire—the desire to be understood.

Our ability to understand is not limited by religion, class, gender, sexuality, or race. It's limited by pride that prevents us from listening well to each other.

Those who can listen well are able to disagree and still love with the kind of love that will cost them something.

In a sense this makes Marie Curie a modern-day prophet. Maybe now is the time that we should seek to understand more so that we may fear less.

However, it is true that we tend to express our fears of others in the form of hatred. Someone who is afraid of foreigners may express that fear through racism. If you're afraid of what the opposing political party might do, you may feel hatred toward that group.

Fear is the bully behind the bully. People who are capable of acts of hatred tend to feel very insecure and afraid, perhaps because they believe others are capable of doing those acts to them. Of course, this is no excuse for hatred, but this gives us a better understanding of why people hate.

To address hatred, we must address fear.

And ultimately, the answer to fear is love.

Fear and love are powerful forces that constantly collide as they seek to influence our daily lives. And too often we allow fear to win. Many people want us to allow fear to prevail, because fear can be used as a tool for control, while love cannot. For the battle to be won, we must learn to overcome fear, and the best way to do that is with love.

Cast Out Fear

Love casts out fear in the same way light casts out darkness. Darkness is the absence of light. Similarly, without love in our lives, we are afraid. Where there is no love, there is fear. We don't know where to turn, and everything seems dangerous. But when we introduce love, it overwhelms the fear. We have something to ground us and show us the way to go, just like a light.

When there is enough love in your life, when you carry love everywhere you go, there is no reason to be afraid. You're no longer focused on the things that scare you. You feel safe and secure knowing you're loved and loving others.

Love can defeat fear when it faces it head-on. Think about the bully who acts out of fear, and the fear they instill in their victims. When you stand up to a bully and decide to act lovingly toward them, you destroy their ability to hurt you. By replacing fear with love, you refuse to allow fear to control you.

We know that people have overcome fear with love. You've likely heard stories of great bravery or self-sacrifice in the name of love—people who have given their lives for friends, mothers who lift cars off their babies, and similar stories. A well-known story that illustrates this is *The Notebook*, in which a husband lovingly cares for his wife who has dementia and no longer remembers him, but he continues to remind her of her past.

Over the next few chapters, we'll dive deeper into how love overcomes fear and how it addresses specific fears.

The Most Powerful Force in the World

It's true—*all you need is love.*

You've heard it hundreds of times from the mouths of celebrities and influencers. You've read it in books and poems. You've seen it in movies and heard it in songs. Turns out they were all right.

That idea had to come from somewhere. We all know somehow that love is vitally important. We desire it like we desire nothing else. It is the greatest thing that gives us joy.

As humans, we are social creatures, and love plays a vital function in our lives. Yet it goes beyond anything science can understand. We all know, deep down, that there's more to love than just a feeling. It has the power to change people, and we believe it has the power to change the world.

People talk about world peace as the loftiest of goals, something that could never be achieved. And they're right—there is too much fear in the world, creating conflict, promoting self-interest, and keeping us from loving. But our culture can change, and while we'll likely never achieve world peace, we can make the world a better place than it is now.

Change starts on an individual level. You can begin by making your own life better by choosing love over fear. This is a process that requires a shift in your thinking, but it is possible to stop living a life of fear by replacing it with love.

The statement "all you need is love" comes with a caveat. The kind of love we're talking about is not what you might think it is.

To accomplish what we need love to do, we first have to define love. The wrong kind of love cannot defeat fear, hatred, or anything else. So, in the next chapter we must do the impossible and definitively answer the question "What is love?"

Make a Difference With Love

Where in your life are people trying to control you with fear? Do you have a boss who bullies you into rushing projects? Do you have a friend or family member who uses fear tactics to guilt you into doing something? What about news outlets who use fear to get you to tune in? Or politicians who use fear to get you to vote for them or follow their political agenda?

Think of a few people who use fear to control you, and write them down:

What would happen if you responded to those people with love? What would change? Would it still have power over you?

Choose one source of fear in your life and respond to it with love.

"Love is not affectionate feeling, but a steady wish for the loved person's ultimate good as far as it can be obtained."

—C. S. Lewis

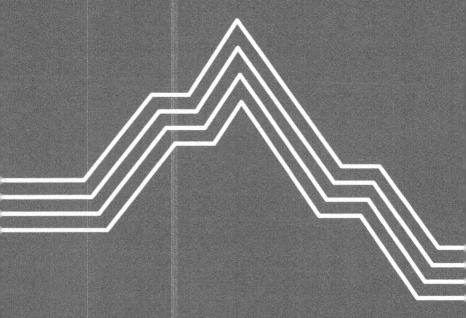

DAY
6

Define Love

Choose five of the following words you most associate with love.

Happiness

Altruism

Experience

Affection

Sex

Selfless

Understanding

Compromise

Partnership

Passion

Diversity

Loyalty

Acceptance

Unity

Fulfillment

Security

Trust

Emotion

Joy

Admiration

Desire

Family

Benevolence

Romantic

The Difficulty in Defining Love

What comes to mind when you think about love?

Chances are it's something romantic.

That is because a majority of what we see and hear through entertainment, marketing, and advertising suggests that love is purely emotional. We know that love is more than *just* an emotion but knowing what that something is can be notoriously difficult.

Love has become more challenging to define today than at any other point in history, and yet this hasn't stopped us from trying to understand it

We're endlessly attracted to love, looking for it in books, music, movies, relationships, and Google searches. But if we set out to define love, where would we start?

The dictionary, of course!

According to the Merriam-Webster online dictionary, love is one of the top 10 most-searched words of all time. This tells us that people are actively trying to figure out what love means. Love is both a noun and a verb, with 13 different meanings that can be summarized as "a passionate affection for a person or thing." You can use the word love to refer to pretty much anything—your close significant other, mac-n-cheese, puppies, and the score of zero in tennis. We would greatly benefit from a narrower definition for the word.

However, this is not an option for us in the English-speaking world, so we must seek to understand love even with all its complexity. Regardless of how difficult love is to define, history reveals our obsession with it.

Sentiments about love often come from some of the most obscure places.

Take for example the famous statement, "It's love that makes the world go round." Ever wondered where that came from? The best we can tell, the 20th century English playwright W.S. Gilbert coined the phrase. Known mostly for his deep influence on American and British theatre, Gilbert is responsible for arguably the most famous phrase about love in history!

Entire historical movements have been driven by ideas about love.

For example, the anti-war counter-culture of the 1960s flew under the banner of "Make love, not war." The late John Lennon championed the slogan as an activist and musician.

As human beings, we can't stop singing about love.

Perry Como, Deon Jackson, and Madonna all believe "Love Makes the World Go Round." Taylor Swift will tell you a "Love Story," and Sara Bareilles will write you a "Love Song." Janet Jackson believes "That's the Way Love Goes," and the Righteous Brothers think "You've Lost That Lovin' Feelin'." Celine Dion believes in "The Power of Love" and so does Huey Lewis. Stevie Wonder might just call "To Say I Love You." Foreigner wants to "Know What Love Is."

Don't we all!

Tina Turner is wondering "What's Love Got to Do With It," and the Bee Gees want to know "How Deep Is Your Love?" The Partridge Family think they love you, but Whitney Houston will "always love you." Beyoncé and Jay-Z are "Crazy in Love." Adele wants to feel her love, and Elvis Presley "Can't Help Falling in Love." Mariah Carey wants a "Vision of Love," but she also knows that "Love Takes Time." Ray Charles couldn't stop loving you, and Queen can't stop talking about a "Crazy Little Thing Called Love." Paul McCartney thinks love songs are silly, so Lionel Richie and Diana Ross must be confused because they believe in "Endless Love."

Is anyone else confused?

If we try to find an appropriate definition for love in popular culture around us, like music, we are bound to be disappointed and misinformed.

Love is also big business—a simple internet search will tell you this. Billions of dollars are spent each year on all things love, which clouds the confusion even further.

The wedding industry is worth roughly $22 billion dollars a year. The average wedding now costs about $25,000. Valentine's Day grosses approximately $30 billion dollars each year—all in the name of love!

Founded by J.C. Hall in 1910, the Hallmark Company is worth $4 billion dollars and employs 30,000 people worldwide. Their mission—to create a more emotionally connected world. At the center of all of it are the Hallmark movies, which gross $600 million in ad revenue by selling their particular brand of love.

The rapidly growing *"Porn Kills Love"* movement from Fight the New Drug (fightthenewdrug.org) is defending love as they push back on the billion dollar worldwide porn industry. With an estimated worth up to $97 billion dollars, porn is responsible for creating more confusion about love because of its dramatic effects on the brain and over-sexualization of relationships.

But it's the current cultural view of love that creates the most confusion. The cultural definition of love is that it *has no definition*.

Love is freely defined however a person *feels* it should be.

So, love can be whatever you wish. But if this is really true, then why do people have such a hard time finding love?

If you can define love however you want, it should be easy to find. Right?

The reason so many people are unhappy, unsatisfied, and full of fear is because they've bought into a counterfeit kind of love—a deception that says love can be whatever you want it to be. If you have bought into it, too, it's not your fault. The deception has become the predominant model of love we're taught throughout our lives. But we must challenge this perspective if we are to grow.

If you want to conquer fear, you must first question your definition of love and come to understand it in a new way. We're going to challenge your ideas of what love is, and you may find this to be a bit uncomfortable.

There are two main problems with the way our culture views love. The first is a lack of agreement on what love means, creating confusion and misconceptions. The second is a result of this inconsistency: we are all looking for love in the wrong places, the vast majority of the time looking for it emotionally in romantic relationships.

While everyone acknowledges that there are multiple types of love, the way we talk about love is usually driven by our desire for romance. But even our interpretation of love through romance is skewed. What we often call love is really just infatuation, a brief moment in time of intense feeling and passion that eventually fades and leaves us wanting.

Without a greater understanding and complete definition for love, our experience of it will be limited. If we want to overcome our fears, we need a definition for love that works, one that can carry all situations and bring substance to our interactions beyond our own self-interest and pleasure-seeking.

We need to expand our view of love.

A New View of Love

If we desire to expand our understanding of love, we must begin with two questions:

First, what's the truest definition of love? And, second, where can we find it?

If love is just a sentiment or a feeling, then you're only going to find it in emotional situations that make you feel good. But is it possible that love can be present even when something makes you feel bad or extremely uncomfortable?

Culture has taught us that we should trust our emotions above all else as the ultimate test for truth and reality. But as we already established with fear, your emotions are a part of your chemistry. They are there to give you signals. They're part of how we interact with the world through instinct and intuition. And your emotions can lead you astray.

Love is more than an emotion, instinct, or sentiment. It is something much greater than that. You probably already know this, though you may not know how to define it fully.

The lack of fulfillment so many of us encounter when it comes to love is because we are judging our *experience* of it purely by the presence or absence of a feeling. This leaves us stuck chasing an emotional high, and when it's not present, disillusion comes and resignation eventually follows.

The secret to developing the fulfilling and lasting effects of love starts with expanding your view beyond emotions to your entire experience of life.

Love is more than an emotion. It is the structure for living all of life.

Have you ever considered love in this way? Have you thought about love as foundational for all aspects of your life?

Just like a skyscraper has steel beams that construct a strong frame to keep it standing when confronted by force or pressure, love creates the same kind of stabilizing force in our lives.

Sounds great! Doesn't it?

When we don't understand something but really want to know more, what do we normally do?

We learn about it.

Terrance Hogan taught middle school at a small school in Tulsa, Oklahoma, for 36 years. Responsible for educating sixth and eighth graders about academics and life, Hogan knew that although his time with each student was short, he could impact them for a lifetime. Throughout his years of teaching, he did just that. At the center of Mr. Hogan's life was love.

If there was one thing he could leave with them that could last and be worth living for, what would it be?

It was a definition for love—one that you could build your life upon. He would recite it in class, add it as a question to tests, and even jokingly threatened that students wouldn't graduate if they couldn't recite it.

For Hogan, love was *knowing, wanting, and doing what is in the best interest of another person.*

We have adopted a form of this definition at the Love and Transformation Institute because we believe it encompasses the fullness of love. It's a definition that requires everything from us for the benefit of those around us.

But just having a right definition doesn't mean that someone will allow it to influence their life the way Mr. Hogan did.

There's a fork in the road we all face on a daily basis: One path seeks to simply experience love and feel loved. The other path is selfless, and it seeks to give love to others. The truth is that these two paths lead to different places, and only one of them is the best one.

The latter path takes more time and costs more energy, but it leads to a much better destination. It requires the time and energy to really think about what is in the best interest of another person and decide if you really want to do what that requires.

What we often don't realize is that the selfless road leads to greater fulfillment and satisfaction, because when you give love and focus on the benefit of another, then they respond in kind. That's where the cycle of love is built.

Real, transformational love must be altruistic, benevolent, and focused on others.

But even in loving others, we are frequently confused by our culture's definition of love. Our culture views love as the following:

1. **Undefined.** Love can be whatever you want it to be. There is no single definition, so your quest for love has no map. How can you know if you've found love if you can't define what it is?

2. **Self-serving.** Because love is about emotions, we seek to experience love rather than to give it. We all want to feel loved, but we're not usually interested in sacrificing our own interests for the sake of making others feel loved.

3. **Conditional.** We're encouraged to abandon those whom we disagree with or those who aren't respectful or kind to us. We love others as long as they've earned it, as long as they don't hurt our feelings, or as long as we agree with their beliefs and their lifestyle.

4. **Undiscerning.** Loving others, by cultural definition, means accepting everything they do or don't believe, because we view love as *conditional*. If love is conditional, then we must only love those who are *acceptable*.

If we view love in these four ways, we come to believe that we must accept everything about a person to be truly loving, making it impossible to love someone who does something wrong or something we disagree with. This belief keeps us from extending love across boundaries of political differences, faiths, or other conflicting belief systems or circumstances. Often, it keeps us from loving those who need it most.

Even though there's no definition for love in our culture, there are descriptions of it. And what these descriptions have in common is that they are self-serving.

What we don't often realize is that *selflessness* is the means by which you receive the greatest personal benefit. But we look at everything through a selfish lens. If we're ever going to experience love and its depth along with the personal benefit that comes from loving, that lens of selfishness has to be shattered.

We must change our definition of love from egoistic to altruistic:

Egoistic love is a love that exists to serve the self, and we think finding it is the answer. But ultimately, it's a shortcut to loneliness and isolation.

Altruistic love is a love that's sacrificial, a love that puts another first. When you do that, you experience satisfaction and fulfillment. It also reciprocates. When you love another selflessly, that love often returns to you.

Love requires not only radical shift in your perception of what love is but also a clear definition for it to function.

Love is to *know*, *want*, and *do* what's in the best interest of *another person*.

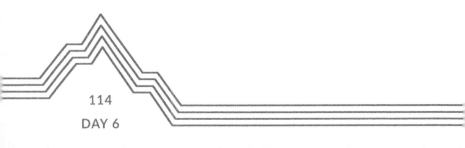

Sacrificial Love

Have you heard the story of the four chaplains on the ship *Dorchester* in WWII? In 1943, the ship was carrying troops through the Labrador Sea when it was hit by a German torpedo and began to sink. Among the chaos of the sinking ship, the four chaplains who were aboard handed out life jackets to the soldiers. When they ran out of life jackets, they gave away their own. As the ship sank, the chaplains linked their arms and went down singing, knowing they had saved at least four more lives.

During a plane crash in 1982, a helicopter came to the rescue of six passengers who had survived and were stuck in the ice water of the Potomac River. As the helicopter dropped a life ring down to them, one of the survivors, Arland Williams, continued to pass it to the other passengers, ensuring that each of them made it to safety before him. When the helicopter came back for him after everyone else had been rescued, it was too late, and he'd died in the freezing water, sacrificing himself for the other passengers.

After the Tohoku earthquake in Japan in 2011, the resulting tsunami killed over 1,500 people. The city of Ishinomaki was destroyed beneath the waves. Hideaki Akaiwa, separated from his family, scuba-dived into the treacherous water, full of debris and dangerous currents, to find his flooded home and rescue his family. He rescued his wife and his mother, and then continued to search for survivors for an entire week afterward.

Also in 2011, a series of floods in Queensland, Australia, forced thousands of people to evacuate their homes. Jordan Rice, aged 13, was in the car with his mother and younger brother when their car was flooded. When someone reached the car to help, Jordan asked for his brother to be saved first. After the younger brother reached safety, the rescuer's rope snapped, and Jordan and his mother both died, but his brother was saved because of his selflessness.

Self-sacrificing stories are told over and over because they touch something deep inside of us. You've experienced this kind of love, a truly selfless love, whether on a large or small scale. You can see how it changes situations and how it moves us.

Have you ever postponed everything at work during an important time to take care of your sick kid? Have you experienced unexpected kindness from a stranger? What about the joy you get from giving something without expecting anything in return?

This kind of love takes initiative and sacrifice. It's not about giving what you wouldn't miss anyway, and it's not just about inconveniencing yourself to hold the door for someone.

We've all experienced this profound type of love in some way, and when we do, it touches our lives. It often catches us off guard. Stories of sacrificial love touch something deep in our hearts. They sometimes make us cry. Even in fictional stories, we are deeply moved by characters who express sacrificial love.

Only self-sacrificial love can break the hardest of all things, which is an angry, bitter human heart. This kind of unbelievable love for another is almost unfathomable. But when we see it, we're moved by it.

Whatever you've been through—whatever has made you hard and left you wanting in a place where you feel like a nobody and nothing can break through— there is something that can heal you. Even if it is not present in your life currently, you can experience profound love.

You have touched it. At moments in your life, you've bumped against it, and it's moved you deeply. You wanted more of it, but maybe you didn't know how to have it or where to find it.

That kind of love can be part of your daily experience. You can give and receive that kind of love.

We unleash the power of love in two ways: by loving and by being loved. Both of those can be difficult. A lot of us are tarnished by our experiences, and we're skeptical and cynical, so we cannot receive love because those who have tried to love us have failed immensely. And our misunderstandings of what love is lead us to look for it in the wrong places.

Selfless love should permeate all parts of our lives and all our relationships— friendships, family relationships, and romantic relationships. Even our professional relationships and our relationships to culture at large (including the way we treat strangers) can benefit from altruistic love.

Love is the solution to so many problems in our culture. We have a crisis of meaning in our society, a crisis of loneliness, a crisis of fear.

Part of the reason it's so hard to find real love is that it can't be manipulated. You have to share it before anybody can experience it and give it back.

You have to take initiative and attempt to do something completely selfless, completely sacrificial, and completely unconditional. In doing so, you will not only experience the joy of loving, but you'll share a little bit of it with the world.

You can't just wait for it to fall on you like a meteor. You have to take action steps and do things that are consciously selfless.

When you do something selfless, how does it make you feel? What is the effect?

What if that feeling and that effect described all your experiences and all your actions? What if you could redirect your life—recalibrate it so that you lived this type of love every day? People would begin to experience you as a loving person, and eventually you would receive that love in return.

Selfless love is transformational. It opens our eyes to others around us, whether we're giving or receiving it. We all understand this kind of love, but we often forget about its power because it's not part of our daily lives.

The Experience of Love

Think of a time someone has done something for you without expecting anything in return, or a time when you did the same for someone else.

What did you feel? Did it change anything? What was the rest of your day like? Write about that experience below or discuss it with someone.

The Love and Happiness Link

There has been a great effort over the past 25 years to explain happiness on a scientific level. We now understand how happiness occurs in the brain. Beyond life circumstances, the same thing makes everyone happy, because we're wired the same way.

What is the key to happiness?

It's altruism. Giving yourself away.

We are naturally social creatures. We're meant to care for each other. Nothing makes us happier than loving one another.

So why, if we understand scientifically how to be happier, do we have a suicide epidemic in the U.S. today?

Even though scientists have studied happiness and understand it better than ever before, people are not becoming happier, and they're not becoming more altruistic.

If you want to be happy, you must understand there is something to be gained through selflessness.

But we must also be careful.

It's purely self-serving to just want to feel good about the good we're doing.

What if you were to discover that you're actually building your own happiness on the backs of other people's suffering?

The reality that our brains respond to doing good puts us in a bit of a challenging position. It sets us up to do good for a payoff.

This would be the dark side of altruism, when we only help others for our own benefit.

True altruism gives and expects nothing in return. While the brain might respond with happy chemicals, this is not the reason that we give ourselves away.

If you're a parent, you know the joy of parental love you experience on Christmas morning. Why are you so excited? You're not getting anything. But it feels so good to give something to your child. You've probably felt the same way giving a gift to a friend or family member.

There is a satisfaction, fulfillment, and a deep sense of meaning that derives from selfless love. We can also gain a sense of adding love and goodness to the world.

What if there was more of that kind of love in the world? What if you could condition yourself to treat others with love as a central focus?

That's how the world changes—one life at a time; one relationship at a time.

It takes sacrifice to do it. You have to get out of your own head, become more aware of others, and stop being so self-preserving. It requires initiative. Somebody has to be willing to go first. True love is always going first.

Embrace a New Look at Relationships

One of the easiest ways to see the misunderstanding of love in our culture is the pervasiveness of hook-up culture. So many people feel compelled to jump around in relationships, searching for the perfect match or for some kind of fulfillment. They're often looking for love by scrutinizing what a partner can provide and whether that partner will make them feel loved the way they desire.

It's easy to blame hookup culture on unrealistic expectations about what romance should look like. But you're never going to find a happy, successful relationship if you go into it looking for self-fulfillment, where your motives are about receiving love rather than giving it.

We use a lot of language in our culture that gives us the wrong impression about real love. English uses many words that associates love with madness. Additionally, many of the words we use are passive: we *fall* in love rather than choosing it. We tend to think of love as something that happens *to* us rather than something we influence and have control over.

In her TED talk "A better way to talk about love," Mandy Len Catron argues that we should look at love as something we create and have to put effort into, like a collaborative work of art. This mindset changes us from acting like passengers or subjects of love's whim and puts us in the driver's seat. We are in control of our relationships. Love takes work, and that work has to be done together, by both parties in a relationship.

A pervasively common myth is that relationships should be evenly weighted—a 50/50 split. You give 50 percent, and so does your partner. You each must compromise, and if you can't meet in the middle, it's over. The problem is that this type of relationship is contractual and conditional.

Love isn't always 50/50. Sometimes love is 100 to zero. In fact, those are the love stories that touch us the most, because deep down we resonate with that kind of love. It's the wife in a vegetative state whose husband tends to her and doesn't leave her side. It's the person who stops to help a stranger fix her flat tire and also gives her money for gas. This kind of love moves us in our souls. It's completely giving. It moves us because it is a more profound kind of love.

We've been taught to believe that unconditional love means we give 100 percent expecting nothing in return.

But you must not expect 50/50 in any relationship, whether it's a romantic partner, a friend, a family member, or a colleague. Sometimes you will give more, and sometimes you will receive more.

Stop keeping a tally.

Just focus on loving the other person as best you can, and chances are your love will be returned to you.

Anything we feel for others that
must be earned, mutual,
or temporal is *not* love.

Call it infatuation, affection,
interest, enjoyment, or whatever,
but don't call it love!

Love, by definition,
is never-ending.

128

Discuss Love

Ask some friends to define love and listen to their responses—how do they describe it? What words do they use? Are they defining real love, or are they operating on a misinterpretation?

You can use this as an opening to begin a discussion about cultural versus altruistic definitions of love. What do your friends think?

"Happiness can be found, even in the darkest of times, if only one remembers to turn on the light."

—**Albus Dumbledore** (from *The Prisoner of Azkaban* screenplay by Steven Kloves)

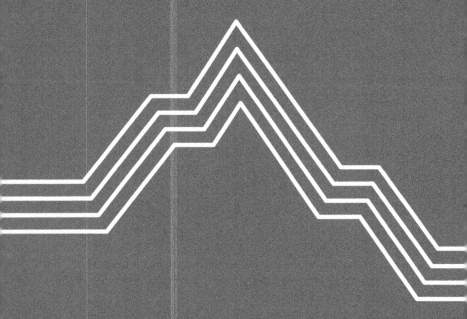

DAY
7

Conquering Your Fear

What if we told you COVID-19 is not the greatest pandemic the world has faced or will face? It's actually fear. Fear is the worst problem we face because it wreaks the most havoc and does the most damage to our personal lives and our culture as a whole. It drives us to do things we wouldn't usually do and keeps us from doing things we normally would. Fear is the biggest epidemic because it undermines and imprisons us, not just for a time, but throughout our entire lives.

Fear that controls us is not our friend. It is our foe. It is like a hostile jail guard that not only keeps us in our cells but also rattles the bars with a stick. It arrogantly saunters back and forth, humming an eerie tune that taunts us day and night. It's always there, never takes it eyes off us, and it robs us of everything good and worthwhile.

Maybe you know this feeling—like someone is watching you, but from the inside. You can feel it in your bones, and it has a tighter grip on you than you are willing to admit. Fear is so powerful. And it never seems to stop. But it isn't unstoppable.

Knowing that fear is always going to be there, there is something you can do about it. There is something you can do to get a little privacy, to take back some control, and to find more joy in your life again. Fear is an ominous enemy, but there are several ways to push back. Here are seven of them.

The first way you can conquer fear is **by knowing it's there.** As it's been said, if you want to defeat your enemy, you have to know your enemy. After all, you can't fight something you don't know is there.

Your enemy, fear, is always lurking, hanging around, and banging on the walls of your soul. It's in the shadows of your heart, and one way to disarm your fear is by seeing it there and shining some light on it. Once it's in the light, it cowers.

The second way you conquer fear is **by identifying your own fears.** What are you afraid of? Failure? Rejection? Being alone? Being broke? Getting sick? Dying? You can strip fear of its power when you name it.

Calling out your fears is a powerful way to make them smaller. Sometimes you just have to name the monsters in the closet so they seem a little less scary. And, if the monsters have names, maybe they will feel a little less like monsters and more like pets.

The third way you conquer fear is **by telling yourself the truth about your fears**. We expend so much emotional energy on the "what ifs" and worry so much about things that never happen. So, instead of wasting energy on what could happen, focus instead on what really is happening.

Freedom from fear comes when you don't give it mental space in your head and emotional energy in your heart. So, take back your internal ground by getting out of your own head and heart and keeping others out too. Your head and heart are holy ground. Don't cede it.

The fourth way you conquer fear is **by focusing on the positive things happening in your life**. It is so easy to get swallowed up by the dark cloud of negative news looming over us. The only way to let the light through is by looking at the good things happening in your life, such as caring relationships, a secure job, or even your physical health!

One of the best ways to overcome the wrong things in your life is by zooming in on the right things. It's been proven that positive thinking changes your attitude and has even been shown to sometimes change your *altitude* too. So, try on optimism and lay off the cynicism for a while.

The fifth way you conquer fear is **by surrounding yourself with the right people.** It's been said that you are the sum average of the five people with whom you spend the most time. If that's true, then you should surround yourself with positive, encouraging people, not negative, disparaging folks.

Shedding toxic people and adding healthy people to your life is essential if you want to be happy. Happiness is contagious, and the best way to contract it is to expose yourself to more joyful people. The bad news is that fear is contagious too, so try to stay away from it. That may mean shutting out sources that try to create more fear in your life.

The sixth way you conquer fear is **by asking for and receiving help from others.** It's been often said that there is strength in numbers. And that is equally true of fear. Scary things aren't so scary when you're not alone.

The secret to thriving in life is relationships. We can't do it alone. If you want to thrive in your travails, then you'll need to have good people traveling with you. None of the roads are as dark when you have company. Having a friend along for the ride helps.

The seventh and most important way you conquer fear is **by developing your appreciation for love in your life.** When you know how to love and be loved, then you will feel safe and secure. And when you truly feel safe and secure, you will not be afraid anymore.

No one who knows that they are fully loved is ever truly afraid. Fear is heightened by isolation and rejection and diminished by love and acceptance. When we know we're fully loved and accepted, we really have nothing to fear.

Fear is a menace, and it is intimidating, but it isn't unstoppable. You can stop or at least slow down the problem of fear in your life by taking back control and doing any or all of these seven things.

Don't be a victim of fear. That enemy is always going to be there, but you can conquer it. You can make it smaller, and you can tame it. Don't let fear rule you and rob you of your happiness. When you learn how to displace fear with love, you will begin to see a dramatic shift in your life.

Displace Fear With Love

Our everyday stress and anxiety is driven by the common foundational fears that we have discussed. Over time, fear can fill up your life like water in a jar. But as you begin to experience more love in your life, it's like slowly adding rocks to that jar. Eventually, the rocks will take up so much space that it will completely displace the water, pushing it out because there is not enough room for both. Love does the same thing to the fear present in our lives. It slowly adds the strength and stable substance we need to our existence, leaving no more room for fear.

But where does the fear come from? Deep down, at the root of it all, there is a lack of love.

No matter what you feel, *you are loved*. You may just not know it.

Maybe you haven't been shown great love, or maybe you've been hurt or betrayed. Maybe you feel mostly loved but still sense something is missing. Maybe you don't know the type of love you're looking for—you've been looking for it in counterfeits, lies of culture, and popular teachings. But what you're looking for is something you'll never find in the type of love our culture celebrates.

We're all looking for something.

We have a need—a gap in our hearts—that aches to be filled. We tell ourselves that if we could just fill it, then we'd finally be happy. We've tried substances, romantic relationships, jobs and titles, money, and experiences to indulge it. And we come up empty.

We're unsatisfied with life.

We feel stressed, anxious, and afraid. We're focused on self—self-preservation and self-fulfillment. And we continue to look for something to satisfy a selfish need, a mysterious hole in our hearts. But the only kind of love that can fill that hole is a love that gives itself away and wants nothing in return.

Love must be authentic and impact all dimensions of your life to defeat fear.

We need an overhaul of love in our lives.

So how does love displace fear?

Let's go back to the five foundational fears. If all fears are rooted in those five instinctual expressions, then we can use them to address fears at their root. Each of these fears may seem massive and unconquerable on its own, but in the face of love, they become manageable. Love opposes each of the foundational fears in a very practical way.

1. In the face of **failure and rejection**, love gives us **acceptance** and a sense of **value**.

2. When we are frightened by the **unknown** and what we cannot predict, love gives us **confidence**. When love permeates your life, you have confidence in yourself, in others, and in a greater sense of meaning and purpose.

3. To address the fear of **pain**, love gives us **comfort**. There is nothing more comforting than love.

4. We fear **isolation**, but love gives us a sense of **belonging** through community and relationship.

5. As we fear **loss of autonomy**, love gives us **purpose** to make our lives and actions meaningful no matter our circumstances.

When you realize that you are fully loved, you experience a greater sense of acceptance, confidence, comfort, belonging, and meaning.

The more these realities are present in your life, the less fear you'll have. As you begin your transformation to maximize love in your life, you'll discover how each of these qualities conquer the foundational fears.

The Love and Trust Link

There is an implicit link between love and trust that must be understood to help displace fear. Our ability to bond to others is essential for love to establish a dependable structure for our lives. Bonding is what forges trust and shapes the way we interpret love.

The great psychologists of the past have expressed their findings about how humans develop in theories designed to explain why we do what we do.

One of the primary explanations is called *attachment theory.*

In attachment theory our ability to love is directly linked to how well our families taught us to bond as children.

Those who learned to functionally bond in a healthy way are able to create secure attachments in their relationships, characterized by safety and trust.

But many of us did not learn a secure form of attachment. As a result, we interpret love through a distorted lens.

In the book *How We Love*, clinical therapists Milan and Kay Yerkovich describe five helpful categories for the way people attempt to love when they did not learn healthy bonding in the early years.

1. Avoider. An avoider is often raised in a home where emotions were not expressed, or were downplayed or devalued, causing a lack of sensitivity to emotional dynamics necessary for bonding.

2. Pleaser. Pleasers are generated by a home where the child is often the source used to satisfy the emotional needs of a parent. Pleasers learn to manage the emotional needs of others around them at the expense of getting their own emotional needs met.

3. Vacillator. A vacillator's experience with bonding as a child can be characterized as unpredictable. As a result, a longing for strong connection develops that feels elusive and as if it will never be satisfied.

4. Controller. The controller is often raised in a traumatic or abusive environment, thus developing a drive to control everything and everyone around them. At times, the controller may use the same abusive behaviors they witnessed growing up to establish control over people or situations they find threatening.

5. Victim. Abusive or traumatic homes also produce victims, who are characterized by an intense drive to avoid chaos and keep the peace, often at a personal cost to themselves.

As you read the descriptions above you may have identified significantly with one of the categories. If so, this can be a great starting point for learning how to bond in a healthy way. Taking this discussion further with a trusted counselor or therapist who understands attachment theory can be a tremendous asset to your growth and ability to trust.

A healthy level of trust allows us to find safety in relying on one another while also discerning when someone is not trustworthy. We can also build trust by extending it to others. Because trust needs to be mutual, someone must take the first step.

Evaluating your trust levels can help you reveal patterns. Are you overly trusting or distrusting? When you understand where your trust or distrust comes from, it can help you determine whether your judgement is reasonable and healthy. From there, you can make conscious decisions about whether or not to extend trust, rather than simply relying on your emotions.

How Much Do You Trust Others?

Strangers: 0——————————————10

Neighbors: 0——————————————10

Colleagues: 0——————————————10

Friends: 0——————————————10

Relatives: 0——————————————10

Family: 0——————————————10

What has caused you to trust or distrust people in each of those categories?

Love Is Like Electricity

If you had to pinpoint one single discovery of human history that caused the greatest amount of change in the shortest amount of time, what would it be?

The wheel? Printing press? Steam engine? Automobile?

We would argue that, hands down, it's electricity.

The ability to harness and deploy electricity as a resource is not very old—only 250 years, give or take. Like many other advancements in history, the discovery of electricity includes a host of interesting characters involved in a march toward infamy. One of those characters is Benjamin Franklin who, in 1752, flew his kite and supposedly discovered electricity. However, some would consider this more lore than fact.

While Franklin is often considered the face of electricity, it was actually an Italian physicist named Alassandro Volta who developed the first power source—a battery known as the Voltaic Pile. The rest is history—literally. Names like Michael Faraday, Nikola Tesla, Thomas Edison, and George Westinghouse all made significant contributions to the future of power.

But on most days, how do we treat electricity? Like everything else that's readily available to us—we take it for granted. And yet, if the power grid ceased to exist tomorrow, smartphones would instantly become paper weights. So many facets of our lives rely on electricity that we are no longer prepared to live without it.

In many ways, we treat love exactly like we treat electricity. We don't give it a second thought until it's gone. Love is like an electrical current flowing from one person to the next. It's empowered in our lives when we give and receive love.

People always use the phrase "the power of love." If you want to know power, you need to understand electricity. Electricity can power factories, airplanes, and space stations. Similarly, love powers the circuit of life. It's what keeps *people* going.

For electricity to work properly, the electrical circuit must be closed. That means the path the electricity travels on—through wires—is a continuous circuit without any breaks. This allows the electricity to get where it needs to go, from one receptor to another. If that path is interrupted, the circuit breaks and the current stops flowing.

We all have ground-fault circuit interrupters (GFCIs) in our homes. When there's a dangerous interruption in the circuit, the GFCI protects us. For example, if you splash water into your outlet, there's a dangerous interruption in the circuit and your GFCI trips to cut off the flow of electricity, requiring you to hit the reset button for electricity to safely be restored.

In our culture, we are experiencing a breakdown in the circuit of love, and it's causing a dangerous interruption. We need to hit the reset button and create a complete overhaul of love.

Reset Your Culture

There is no doubt that our culture has a deficiency of love.

Madeleine L'Engle, author of *A Wrinkle in Time*, lamented, "We have much to be judged on ... slums and battlefields and insane asylums, but these are the symptoms of our illness and the result of our failures in love."

What is our "illness"? The absence of love in our lives and relationships.

It's not too late to reset. There is time to pivot.

There's a tipping point, and it's not out of reach. For any culture to change, only 10 percent of its population must believe in something.

What if 10 percent of people began to live with authentic and substantial love? The kind of love that informs all of life. The change would be massive!

So many people have an underlying feeling of worthlessness. They've been made to feel that way by others and by their own fear and self-doubt. There is also a movement in our culture today to value some over others as affirmation of the common good.

Love is built upon the fundamental agreement that all human beings matter and that every human being has worth. Therefore, everyone is lovable and worthy of love.

We must accept this as truth to experience authentic love at a personal and a cultural level.

Why is it so important to recognize the inherent worth of every human?

It drives how we view our world, how we treat other people, and how we lead our organizations.

It's not possible to fully experience authentic love—to allow it to take root in our relationships and our culture—until we come to agree on the bottom line that all human beings are worthy of love.

Why do we have such visceral reactions to racism, human trafficking, domestic violence, rape, and abuse? Because we know it is an affront to the dignity of a human being. Deep down, we know that humans have inherent worth. But do we have the same kind of visceral reactions to agendas that manipulate under the banner of what's best for all of humanity, agendas that are built on the backs of real suffering and seek to exclude rather than include?

We have to confront the stigma that there are some human beings who are worth more than others. We must destroy this idea for the current of love to be restored.

The most powerful transformation a person will ever experience comes from learning to be a more loving person. The way to do that is to recognize the value of another human being.

Furthermore, you must believe that by loving another person, you're adding value and good to their life and to the world. The goal is to be the kind of person who is consistently making deposits of love but no withdrawals. The result is an investment that grows exponentially, producing more returns that can bear greater and greater profits.

Understanding love in this way is drastically different than what we generally hear affirmed by society. You've been encouraged to "pay it forward," and that this is the way to change culture. Do good for others because good has been done for you. What we're encouraging here is radically counter to that mindset. The model of love we affirm is built on making a contribution. It's giving without expecting anything in return. It's a lifestyle with only one agenda—add to the foundation of love needed to actually change the world.

Sometimes you may experience good that comes back around related to something that you did. But it's important to recognize that love is not an equal exchange—you won't receive an act of love for every loving thing you do. But you'll get a profound return through the joy of establishing a loving lifestyle in all dimensions of your life.

By becoming more loving, we can begin to make a difference and transform our culture.

How Has Love Shaped You?

Identify three positive experiences you've had that have been formative or shaped who you are. Write them below or talk about them with someone.

1.

2.

3.

Tap Into the Power

In order to conquer fear, you must be willing to transform. It requires action and change in your worldview and lifestyle.

Maturity and transformation happen through becoming a more loving person. Characteristics come out of love like kindness and patience. These characteristics are developed and built over time. Transformation is not something that happens overnight. It takes work, and you have to continue to make an effort, day after day.

First, you must recognize that you are worthy of love.

Simply because you exist, you are worthy of dignity.

You are worth loving.

There's nothing you have to do beyond just *being*.

You don't have to earn love.

Your worth doesn't diminish because other people fail to see it.

You are lovable.

It's important to recognize that about other people as well.

Every human being is lovable and worthy of love.

Love is built upon the fundamental agreement that all humans have worth. We cannot change our culture until we agree on this.

To begin to love authentically, you must accept that you are worthy of love, and then you must extend that worth to everyone else.

This may be a challenge—there are probably plenty of people you don't think are worth loving. But in order to create change in ourselves and in our culture, we must acknowledge the inherent dignity and worth of every human. This is what will allow us to love and to let go of fear.

The next step is to act in love.

Kindness is not the absence of meanness. It is an expression of selfless love.

Seek ways to be kind to others. In doing so, you will make the world a more loving place, and you will help others become less fearful as well. By recognizing and loving others, you're contributing to the wellbeing of the human race, and you're making a difference and adding value to the world.

Transformation happens by becoming a more loving person. If your transformation process is rooted in your own success, you'll never be truly happy.

Finally, you must learn to accept love from others in return without expecting it. You may not receive value in return, but you must learn to give love despite everything.

St. Augustine once wrote that now famous Latin phrase "Amor meus, pondus meum," which is translated as "my love is my gravity." Gravity is the force that holds us to the ground much like love holds down our fear.

Love is heavy, and it is weighty. It stabilizes us and allows us to impact the world around us. Just like physical weight, it allows us to change things in the physical world. So, think of it this way: you can throw your weight around with love and make a difference. After all, if fear can be weaponized, so can love. So, let's wage love.

Transform

Take a few minutes to answer the following questions. You can make a list, write out your thoughts, or discuss the questions with someone you trust. If you're into mindfulness, think about love during meditation.

How would my life be different if I truly believed I was worthy of love?

How would my community change if everyone were treated as worthy of love?

"Our culture has accepted two huge lies. The first is that if you disagree with someone's lifestyle, you must fear or hate them. The second is that to love someone means you agree with everything they believe or do. Both are nonsense. You don't have to compromise convictions to be compassionate."

—**Rick Warren**

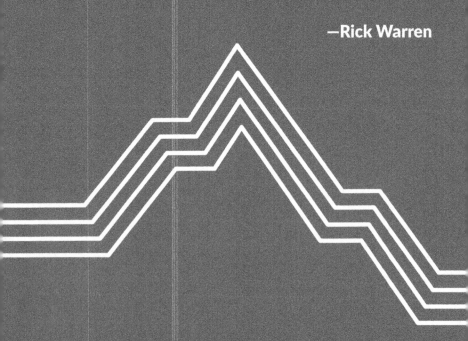

DAY
8

Study the Circuit - Redefine Love

Clues:

1. Desire to do good to others; an act of kindness; a charitable gift

2. A person attached to another by feelings of affection or personal regard

3. Characterized by or indicative of pleasure, contentment, or joy

4. Faithfulness to commitments or obligations

5. A longing or craving, as for something that brings satisfaction or enjoyment

6. Oneness of mind, feeling, etc., as among a number of persons

7. Any powerful or compelling emotion or feeling

8. Full of mental distress or uneasiness because of fear of danger or misfortune

9. The behaviors and beliefs characteristic of a particular group of people

10. Something that causes a person to act in a certain way, do a certain thing, etc.

11. Physical, mental, or emotional strain or tension

12. To torment oneself with or suffer from disturbing thoughts

13. Freedom from danger, risk, care, anxiety, or doubt; well-founded confidence

14. The emotion of great delight caused by something exceptionally good or satisfying; keen pleasure

15. The principle or practice of unselfish concern for or devotion to the welfare of others

15. A feeling of wonder, pleasure, or approval

16. A settlement of differences by mutual concessions

17. Any strong agitation of the feelings actuated by experiencing love, hate, fear, etc., and usually accompanied by certain physiological changes

18. An emotional or other connection between people

19. A group of people or things that are related by common characteristics, features, or properties

19. Anticipation of the possibility that something unpleasant will occur

20. Strong predilection, enthusiasm, or liking for anything

21. Confident expectation of something

22. Intense dislike; extreme aversion or hostility

*Answer key on page 357

Think of a time when you felt deeply loved, or a time when you felt a great amount of love for someone. What did you feel in that moment?

Acceptance

Confidence

Comfort

Belonging

Purpose

Does the feeling you chose on the previous page directly combat your primary fear type?

Acceptance > failure and rejection

Confidence > the unknown/unpredictable

Comfort > pain

Belonging > isolation

Purpose > loss of autonomy

Whether or not the moment of love you identified overwhelmed the fear you felt at the time or are currently experiencing, it was not a moment of fear. Identifying parts of your life that mean a great deal to you or that had an impact on you helps you better understand your own fears. It also helps you know what you may need to focus on during your transformation to love better and to defeat fear.

Be the 10 Percent

The book *Trillion Dollar Coach* chronicles the work of Bill Campbell, who is arguably the most successful coach to executives in history. His list of clients is dominated by the Silicon Valley who's who, including Steve Jobs (Apple), Eric Schmidt (Google), Jeff Bezos (Amazon), and Sheryl Sandberg (Facebook). As a former football coach, Campbell applied his principles to those building the most powerful companies of our age—companies that would irreversibly influence culture. What was at the center of Bill's methodology?

Love.

Clients Schmidt, Rosenberg, and Engle had this to say about Campbell's approach:

> *"So this is what we learned from Bill: that it's okay to love. That people in your team are people, that the whole team becomes stronger when you break down the walls between the professional and human personas and embrace the whole person with love."*

Sounds like an amazing way to run a company—doesn't it?

However, while these Silicon Valley firms were growing by leaps and bounds, there was an equally consequential crisis developing in our society.

That crisis was and still is suicide. From 1999 to 2019, the suicide rate increased 33 percent, and it became the second leading cause of death for people ages 10-34, according to the CDC.

While Bill Campbell was coaching countless tech executives riding the wave of wild success, society was fracturing.

It's important to consider what role these companies and their products have played in the increase of epidemics like suicide across the landscape of our culture. Did love go beyond how the companies were operating to what they were producing? Was love a part of the conversation related to the imprint that would be left on the world? Or was love just being exchanged among those grossing billions in revenue? Did they consider whether their operations were in the best interest of the common good?

Crisis creates urgency—and we're in a crisis. We have a crisis of meaning and a crisis of loneliness. We have national epidemics of anxiety, depression, and suicide. But by and large, people suffer silently in this crisis.

People are starting to talk more about mental health, but that's not necessarily the final solution to the crisis. We may be able to treat mental health problems, but the fact that the rates of anxiety, depression, and suicide are so high in the first place indicates something is wrong with our culture.

We've reached a point in history unlike any in the past. People feel incredibly insecure and afraid.

It's clear that change is necessary.

What would it take to change our culture, to live in a culture that's driven by love rather than fear?

It would take embracing a definition of love that makes sense and actually works—one that helps us be able to not only know, want, and do what's in the best interest of another person, but to also know, want, and do what's in the best interest of the common good!

The tipping point in any society is 10 percent.

According to scientists at the Rensselaer Polytechnic Institute, only 10 percent of a population needs to believe in something to change a culture. Director Boleslaw Szymanski says, "When the number of committed *opinion* holders is below 10 percent, there is no visible progress in the spread of ideas. However, once that number grows above 10 percent, the idea spreads like flame."

So, the question is this: Will you be part of the 10 percent?

Invest in Love

You only have one life—how will you spend it?

When it comes to money, we only want to invest it in something that will give us a return. We need to think about our lives in the same manner. What is worth investing your life in?

Some investments are worth making while others are not. So, when it comes to investing in love, how can you tell the difference?

To combat the crisis our culture is facing, it's going to take people who consciously choose to invest in love—the kind of love that makes a real difference and is not compromised by personal agendas or hijacked by passing cultural fads. This kind of love is uncomfortable. It stands up against cultural norms and also challenges dangerous ideas pushing for change. It does not tell you what you want to hear and does not believe that anything goes. The only way for love to truly take root in your life is when *you* stop using it and *it* starts using you.

Love must become a calibrating force in your life and for it to do that, it cannot be defined by you. It has to be bigger than you and beyond you. This may sound like common sense and that's because something inside us tells us that we really don't know everything.

If someone approached you on the street and told you they had figured out exactly how to define love and happiness, what would you say to them?

Chances are you would probably say nothing and walk away thinking they are mentally unstable.

And yet this is the predominant way that we approach defining the most important concepts in life. We believe they are defined by self.

This also creates a significant problem. What if our definitions of love are different and contradict each other? Then who is right? If everyone is creating their own definition for love, how will anyone ever know if they are truly being loving? Complete communication breakdown is often the result.

Self-defined love is a risky and often costly investment because it has no other guiding force than itself. When that is the case, how will you ever be able to tell if the investment is worth making?

It's easy to throw around the idea of love as a solution to many of our problems. But seeing it make a substantive difference in our lives and culture is a different matter. We need a new investment strategy.

Even when we acknowledge the need for more love, we typically don't know where to start. There are a couple of things that must happen in order to become more loving.

First, you must recognize the need for change within *yourself.*

Changing the world doesn't begin by asking others to change.

Have you noticed that you can't make others change? That is because people rarely do what other people tell them to do. They mostly do what they tell themselves to do. You cannot make others change without setting an example and living out what you believe.

This is why what we believe about love is so critical. As we stated earlier in this book, we need to think differently about love. Until love becomes the calibrating force in our lives and culture, we will continue to struggle to see significant change. That is because we don't know what we're headed toward. There is nothing that stands outside of us to provide us direction. We must have something to measure love against that tells us whether it really is love or not.

In order for the world to change, people must learn to change their minds. That starts with you. You're allowed to change your mind. You are free. And to become a less fearful person, you *must* change.

It's not too late to change your trajectory and your philosophy of life—to recalibrate everything by changing the way you think about love.

In a culture that claims to be free, we're so often told exactly what we're supposed to think. Here's permission to think again, to think for yourself. Stop listening to what you're supposed to think and take the time to think through matters for yourself.

Let's actually try it.

How would your life be different if you truly believed in love that works?

Ask yourself the following:

- How would the world be different for me if I truly believed I was worthy of love?

- How would my relationships change if I treated other people as worthy of love?

- How can changing the way I love advance the common good?

- How would my community function differently if people actually loved each other in a substantive way?

Give this some thought. How would your life be better and different? How could your relationships be better? How could your community and your culture be different if we all spent some time considering the importance of love?

We're asking you to pivot, and that requires recalibrating your mind and your heart toward a new kind of living.

Recalibrate

Metanoia is an ancient Greek concept meaning a transformative change of heart. In order for love to change your life, you must go through a transformation of love. That transformation begins by knowing where you are in reference to where you are going.

Establishing what you believe about love is the first step to becoming more loving. One of the most challenging thoughts you could ever consider is that what you believe about love might be wrong. What if what you believe has actually been harmful rather than helpful?

If you want to effectively grow in love, you need to understand where you're starting. This is a part of the recalibration process. You must deconstruct before you can reconstruct and see love in a new way.

- What have you been taught about love?

- What do you believe about love?

- What are your deficiencies in love?

You may have already identified the answers to some of these questions in the exercises you've done so far. Go back and look at the exercises you've completed, and then use the space below to reflect on your answers to the questions above.

What have you been taught about love?

What do you believe about love?

What are your deficiencies in love?

The Condition of Love

On previous pages, we have used the term *unconditional* multiple times to refer to love.

Do you believe in unconditional love? If so, why?

Consider the concept of unconditional love for a moment—how do you understand it?

We tend to believe unconditional love is achievable by simply setting our desires aside and choosing to accept others. We think this means that we must ignore an offense, a disagreement, or a conflict.

We tell ourselves, "Just love them unconditionally."

The term unconditional means without limitation. It's a love that is not limited by personal beliefs, cultural whims, forced philosophies, or passing fads. But it is more than that.

Unconditional love is perfect love. Absolute love. A love without reservation.

It is an exposing love. One that reveals what is true, good, and beautiful.

It's a love that is not left to our own whims and opinions. Instead, it is a rock upon which all of our ill-conceived ideas and notions of it crash.

But here's the problem: we live in a culture that is confused about unconditional love. The unconditional love that we *want* always believes us, accepts all of our flaws, and does not require us to change. It's the proverbial Hallmark view of love.

Here's how it sounds: "If you love me, you'll accept me, and allow me to do whatever I wish."

The flip side of this mentality is harsh and at the root of much of the division in our society today. It says, "If you don't allow me to do whatever I wish, then you don't accept me and thus you don't love me—you actually hate me."

This perception of love is short on commitment, endurance, and sacrifice because it's based purely on self-fulfillment. It's meant for receiving, not contributing. And it may not really be love at all.

Loving selflessly is the only way to love genuinely.

The truth is that your efforts to love will not last if they are rooted in selfish desires. Selfishness is a condition—a limitation to love. But because we live in such a self-serving society, it's often difficult to identify how deeply our self-focused view of love runs. We promote ourselves, defend ourselves, and protect ourselves at all costs. And when our selfish desires are challenged, we play the trump card of "love."

Have you tried to love unconditionally? Did you find it difficult?

It could be that you're trying to do something that you can't actually do. Unconditional love is a paradox. It is based on the *condition* that there is no limit to how far it can go.

When we try to define love ourselves, our thoughts and feelings about love set limitations for what love can and can't do. This is partly because we are unable to consider all of the implications of love, its impact, and its power. We also live with a strong cultural message about what love should and won't do. Unconditional love is hard for us to achieve because *we* are a limitation.

This limitation is revealed in our thoughts and actions. All thoughts and actions are either loving or they're not, and this is not dependent on how we feel about them. Have you ever had to apologize for doing something you initially thought was right but turned out to be wrong? If you could truly define love for yourself and still love others unconditionally, then you would never make this mistake. You would love perfectly in every situation all of the time.

The place we must begin is acknowledging our limitations when it comes to love and admitting that love is something we don't do very well.

Love must be learned and developed, which means we are all students—not experts, and therefore not capable of defining it ourselves or loving perfectly all the time. Hopefully, this is a relief, because it's a heavy responsibility to love unconditionally in a world with so much hatred, division, and pain.

That doesn't mean you shouldn't feel good about trying to love people selflessly. Joy is established through selflessness. If your motives and corresponding kindness are genuine, then your love will translate.

Another cultural mantra, "Kindness is everything," is what we should be after. We know how difficult it is to love unconditionally, so when we find it challenging to love someone, our solution instead is to be kind.

This approach works because kindness is a choice. You can choose to be kind even when you find it challenging to love. And in a sense, that kindness is an expression of love, even though there are limitations to your love.

But spreading the love and kindness that we are discussing takes resolve. You may not see the return on your investment for every loving action you take. Sometimes it may even hurt to deny yourself in order to extend love to others, especially if they are ungrateful or even resistant.

And some people *are* resistant and ungrateful. They haven't been taught to recognize love because they harbor a great deal of resentment or disbelief. What happens when they are ungrateful or resist your expressions of love and sacrifices?

The answer is simple, though it may be difficult: love doesn't stop. If you're truly loving, you are still committed.

This isn't easy. Sometimes it takes weeks, months, or even years to see a return on your kindness. In fact, in some cases, you may continue to invest in someone and never see a return.

But your actions still contribute good to the world and to that person's life. Just because they don't recognize it now doesn't mean they never will. Does their lack of gratefulness take away the sense of satisfaction that you feel from doing what's right?

There's a sense of joy and fulfillment that comes from loving sacrifice. And people who live an altruistic life are immensely joyful. In fact, you would be hard pressed to find anyone who regrets living a life defined by selfless love.

Your Perception of Love

Think of a time when you did something selfless out of love for someone. What was their reaction? How did it affect you? Talk about the experience with a friend or write about it here.

"Every man must decide whether he will walk in the light of creative altruism or in the darkness of destructive selfishness."

—**Martin Luther King Jr.**

DAY

9

Transformational Love

We've discussed in detail the challenge of under-standing love, so now let's move forward in exploring the kind of love that works. The love that will conquer our fear. At LTI we call this transformational love. It is love that propels change and acknowledges the process of growth as well as the limitations we face in our journeys to become loving people. Shifting our view of love from unconditional to transformational replaces unrealistic expectation with helpful structure and direction for learning how to love.

Transformational love engages through thought, desire, and action.

It is to know, want, and do what's in the best interest of another person and the common good. It's the desire to see your relationships to individuals and all of humanity transformed by love.

How do you understand the best interest of someone else? We can't always know what's in someone's best interest because we aren't able to predict the future and don't know everything about someone's life. But, by loving someone with transformational love, you can love them better than they love themselves, and their best interests become much clearer. And here's the thing: everyone is capable of loving in this way!

How can you recognize the transformative influence of love in your life? What does it look like? The following are five characteristics that will help us develop this kind of love.

Kind

Love is kind to others. Kindness has become somewhat of a litmus test in our culture as to whether someone really cares. But what is kindness really?

Kindness is not simply the absence of cruelty. It is extending favor purely for the benefit of another person.

Kindness also helps us authenticate love. It is woven into a person's demeanor and approach to life. When someone is kind, we can tell that the virtue of kindness has been formed in their character.

Kindness is also a way you can assess yourself. When people experience you, would they say that they have encountered someone who is kind? Kindness celebrates favor given to others without consideration of self or of getting anything in return.

In essence, kindness is rooted in a genuine and sincere consideration for the well-being of others.

Absolute

Transformational love possesses an absolute quality.

The word *absolute* means complete and free from imperfection. Because love is perfect, it has the ability to drive out fear and establish a realistic plumb line for growth. It permeates every part of our lives. Love that transforms brings wholeness where there is brokenness, healing where there is separation, and reconciliation where there is conflict. That is because real love is grounded in reality and does not change. Instead, it creates change.

We have chosen to use the word *real* to modify love here because our world is full of counterfeit love—fluid and unstable love that is really not love at all. The truth is that some thoughts, desires, and actions are unloving even though we may try to convince ourselves otherwise. You see, love is not altered by our ideas about it. Transformational love constantly reveals qualities that create health and growth. But for it to do so, it must be a stable lens through which we view reality.

The idea of real love creates tension for many people because they believe they have more control over defining reality than they actually do. The truth that we cannot define reality shows up in life through very unfortunate situations when reality hits us harshly in the face, caring little about how we feel. Suffering, tragedy, and trauma contribute to all of our lives in seemingly cold and emotionless ways. It takes something transformative to process these experiences when things just don't make sense. We need something reliable and unchanging. The absolute quality of love is the only thing that can bring clarity where there is confusion and provide a solid foundation for living. It does not require or expect anything it return. It gives regardless of circumstances or how the recipient responds. It does not discriminate, but it is discerning.

Absolute, transformational love extends to everyone, and it provides space to carry both the good and the bad. It does not excuse wrongdoings and keeps loving regardless of circumstances.

Patient

Love that transforms is willing to wait for a response. As you grow in patience, your ability to love without limits increases. It means that you continue to love even when it's difficult to do so, even when change seems like it may never come.

It also means extending patience to others when it causes you inconvenience and being understanding of circumstances that affect everyone differently. Patience gives others the benefit of the doubt. It means believing the best of others and not assuming the worst.

When you understand that everyone struggles with knowing how to love, you begin to recognize how complex the lives of others are. The transformative effect of patience gives you the ability to love when someone cuts you off in traffic or insults you during tense encounters at work or in school. Patience ultimately adds to your ability to extend help and kindness to others, which can contribute to their growth.

Transcendent

Transformational love extends beyond life, and it's why we memorialize those whose legacy of love continues even after they have passed. Teresa of Calcutta is a vivid example of how love transcends when it transforms. Her love endured well beyond the point where most would have stopped.

According to Teresa, if love stops, by definition, it is not love. We're hollow if we think we love someone and then stop loving them. People often choose to stop loving because they simply don't want to. Love in its essence is eternal, and recognizing its transformational quality means there is no limit to its application. Even time is no exception as a condition.

Where people often get confused is that they believe love is only an emotion. If the emotion goes away, they think they must have stopped loving. Love is not based on emotion. Affection can come to an end, but not love. If you base love on emotions, it will fade. If it's not love, it might be infatuation, preference, affection, affinity, or romance. Some people say they fall in and out of love. That's only romance—feelings of attraction and fondness. It's an indication that transformational love was not at the center of that relationship. No one falls in and out of love if they understand that love is permanent.

Forgiving

In order for love to transform, it must also forgive. That is because forgiveness respects the freedom that we all have to disagree or offend. When someone hurts you, do you give up on loving them? If so, you're limiting love's ability to change the relationship.

Forgiveness is one of the greatest skills a person can develop. So, what is forgiveness? It means you are no longer holding a debt over someone's head. You let go of whatever that person did to wrong you. It gives freedom to you and the other person.

Forgiveness doesn't come easily to many people. You may want to forgive but not know how to go about doing it. How do you know if you've truly forgiven someone?

Ask yourself if you feel free, or are you still carrying the burden?

Reflect on Transformational Love

Kind

Do you consider yourself to be a kind person? If so, what acts of kindness do you practice on a regular basis? How often do you go out of your way to do something for someone else without any obligation or expectation of return?

Absolute

How does the concept of love as reality change the way it functions in your life?

Patient

Who is the most patient person you know? Describe how you have seen them display patience in various circumstances.

Transcendent

How easily do you connect with the concept of love's transformational qualities being something bigger than you and beyond you? Have you experienced this phenomenon?

Forgiving

Write about a time when you've seen or experienced the release of an offense and the restoration of freedom that came through forgiveness.

Know Love's Purpose

Our ability to fully understand the purpose of love is entirely dependent upon recognizing the transformational effects that love can have on all dimensions of life—not just our relationships. Love is more than a universal language or something that bonds us together; it is the operating system upon which culture runs.

The purpose of love is to transform culture.

Love is the most powerful force in the universe in the way it can transform people, organizations, and entire societies. We have the opportunity to participate in that change by allowing love to shape and empower every aspect of our lives.

Perhaps the most evident example of love fulfilling its purpose is through family. When parents intentionally shape the culture of a home with love, not only do the children flourish, the parents do as well. Their loving culture also extends beyond them to everyone who enters that home or encounters someone from that family. Culture inside the home travels to the outside through those who are formed by it. Families are a dynamic expression of transformational love, and building a culture that raises

195

DAY 9

loving children is one way we can influence the world around us.

For many people, their home is the greatest contribution they will make to the world. There is great fulfillment to be found in building a solid home structure that contributes to the common good. But what if we could extend that love beyond our own homes to transform the culture at large?

This is where our understanding of family and community are critical. Many people are looking for a place to belong. Often, they look for it at work. After all, most of us spend 75 percent of each day working, and we do that for over 75 percent of our lives. If we are not able to experience transformative love in the workplace, then we are not finding what we are looking for.

The role that love can play in transforming the workplace is usually overlooked and undervalued. A workplace shaped by love will treat situations very differently than a workplace shaped by data, metrics, and productivity. This is a big problem in our culture. Overall, we're very metrics-driven rather than love-driven. People are attributed value based on their productivity rather than based on their worth as human beings.

What if you viewed your employees or co-workers as family members? Many workplaces claim to do so but don't follow through on the commitment to love those people. You don't give up on family members, on people you love. When your kid acts up, throws a hissy fit, or runs away from home, you don't kick them out of the family. But that's not how it usually is in the workplace. When an employee steps out of line or gets into trouble, they're normally fired from the "family."

In our culture, it has become too easy to discard relationships. What we need is the transformational nature of love to change this.

How would your relationship to your work environment change if all of the interactions there were based on love?

When we begin to extend transformational love to people in our everyday lives, we will start to see the kind of change we're looking for.

Shape Culture

We are all active in shaping culture. Each of us has a sphere of influence, which may include our homes, workplaces, and communities. Setting out to create large-scale cultural change may be unrealistic for most people. However, we can all impact the people and places in our spheres of influence.

The starting point for many people is through teaching our children to be loving. If you're a parent or if you want to be a parent someday, stop for a moment and ask yourself these questions: What are you actually passing on? Are you passing on a legacy of love that transforms? *Why* do you have or want kids?

Shaping culture is not an option. Through the way you live, you are constantly making deposits into culture, whether you like it or not. And those deposits add up to something. The cumulative effect of our contributions to this world is why it's so important for us to consider how we can become more loving.

Every one of us has a strong desire for unity and connectedness. It is one of the major reasons we search for romantic partners. People are still getting married. In a world where you could argue that marriage is obsolete, people still choose it.

What is this innate desire to get married, to have children, to build a life, and to develop friendships? It's our internal drive to create and shape culture.

Deep down in all of us, there is a desire to create a culture where we can experience the transformational power of love. And each of us can begin to see this reality take shape when love becomes the driving factor behind how we live our lives.

Even if you don't want what we've talked about specifically, you probably still want the same result in other ways. For example, even if you don't want to get married, you still have a desire for companionship and close friendships. Even if you don't want to have children, you still have a desire to care for things. Maybe it's animals. Maybe it's a philanthropic project.

The need to extend love to others and to shape culture is innate in all of us—you were made for it.

At the core, you are a lover.

You will feel incomplete if you don't have and give love.

When it's done right, transformational love is not fleeting. It becomes our greatest tool for finding purpose. We all have a need for it, and we're always trying to fill that need with all sorts of things. But the only thing that will satisfy that need is creating a home and a culture filled with relationships that have been transformed by love. You can't satisfy that need by building a house or making money or creating a name for yourself. Those things are unsatisfying because they're not relational.

Satisfying your need for love cannot be done solely through action. You can't go out just to do good and feel completely satisfied. It has to become deeply personal and purposeful.

So how can you extend that love to shape culture? How can you give that love to your neighbor, your coworker, or your employee?

When you expand your view of love beyond an emotion to a transformative way of living, it changes everything! You orient your life to it, and it becomes the thing you are passionate about. Naturally, you'll want to share it with others. When people come into your sphere of influence, they'll want to experience the same kind of love that is transforming you.

Some people orient their lives to being successful or self-preserving. But you can choose to make love central to your life and, in doing so, choose to create and shape culture.

If you do, you won't be able to lay love back down—it will become the very theme of your life.

When this is done right, it distances you from the cultural perception of love as an emotion, and love becomes a catalytic agent in your life. It doesn't come and go. Instead, it establishes itself as a consistent current on which your life runs and continually invites others to join.

Your Sphere of Influence

Use the circle below to create a visual representation of your sphere of influence. What people and places do you interact with? What kind of impact would transformational love make for each of these people or places?

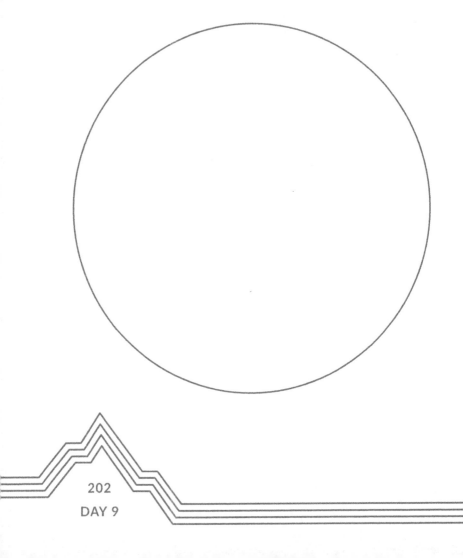

"Where there is love there is life."

—**Mahatma Gandhi**

DAY
10

How Loving Am I?

Love accounts for the interests of others as well as your own interests in a balanced way. We all naturally consider ourselves, but how much do you also consider others in your daily thoughts, desires, and actions? Be honest with yourself and mark on the scales below how you would score the balance between your interests and the interests of others.

People different than you:

Self 0——————————————10 Others

Neighbors:

Self 0——————————————10 Others

Colleagues:

Self 0——————————————10 Others

Friends:

Self 0——————————————10 Others

Relatives:

Self 0——————————————10 Others

Family:

Self 0——————————————10 Others

Next, choose three categories from the list above. Then write a short description of how you could begin loving well by considering the interests of that particular group more.

What Is a MEGALIFE?

MEGA simply means great. And great means remarkable in magnitude, degree, or effectiveness.

Building a MEGALIFE is driven by the desire to live the greatest life possible. It acknowledges that greatness is not quickly or easily attained but built with a lot of effort over time.

A MEGALIFE is developed through a process of discovery and experimentation combined with a relentless pursuit of growth. It accounts for the past but sees a different future. It's a life full of meaning, value, and substance. It rejects the allure of a self-preserving, pleasure-seeking lifestyle for the stable contentment of a life constructed intentionally. It's a life full of realized potential delivered over time. A MEGALIFE can be designed anytime, anywhere, and by anyone. And, most importantly, MEGALIFE is available to all!

At LTI, we believe the following to be true: everyone desires to live their greatest life but very few know how to do it.

Would you agree?

To begin building a MEGALIFE takes a shift in perspective and a new identity.

A New Perspective

You must redefine success as growth instead of achievement and seek meaning instead of influence as the ultimate outcome. A MEGALIFE is more about who you are becoming, not about what you are accomplishing.

Become a Growth Junkie

There is a growing community of people just like you who desire to live a MEGALIFE. We call them "growth junkies," and you are invited to join us. Growth junkies see everything in life as an opportunity for growth and believe that growth is the currency of meaning. The end goal for growth junkies is to become the most loving people we can possibly be!

Will you grow with us?

The Process of Transformation

A process is defined as a continuous action, operation, or series of changes taking place in a definitive manner. Transformation, like many other worthwhile endeavors in life, is a process. It involves stages that work in conjunction with each other to produce the outcomes that we desire.

There are four phases to the transformation process:

Awareness > Information > Integration > Transformation

Having a structured approach for the transformation process is tremendously helpful for engaging in the work it takes to see lasting change. Each stage will assist you in developing a foundation for your personal growth.

Awareness

The first stage involves identifying a wound or area of brokenness in your life. This often surfaces through character deficiencies we discover when life is overwhelming or through facing a crisis. It's when the heat gets turned up in life that we become aware of our opportunities for growth.

For example, someone might enter into a period of high stress in the workplace, and it reveals their irritability and a lack of patience. A person who values growth and has a great sense of awareness will choose to see this as a chance to develop their character when many others would explain it away as a fluke or an "off" day.

Information

Once someone becomes aware of an opportunity for change, information is needed to grow. We don't often understand what we're dealing with and sometimes need help to make sense of the need for change. Often just a little research or a few conversations with trusted individuals can give us what we need for the third phase—integration.

Integration

You can view integration as a bridge to cross—one that you will cross over, come back across, and sometimes get stuck in the middle. That's because integrating a new way of life can be incredibly complex and challenging. But don't be dismayed. Discouragement is often a sign that the transformation process is working. As you become better at something, you're better able to recognize the ways in which you still fall short. Ultimately, this will help you grow if you stick with it.

Transformation

The final phase of transformation is the outcome of the other three phases. It's a byproduct of all the time, effort, experimentation, and commitment given to your overall approach to change.

Find the Short Circuit

We often take for granted things readily available to us in life. Rarely do we give them a second thought as we go about our days.

Take electricity for example. It is a blessing that powers our entire lives, but when there is a problem, your smartphone can become a paper weight in a hurry. Short circuits are one of the most common electrical problems that cause dangerous events, which interrupt the flow of the electrical current. If they're not handled correctly, these kinds of issues can potentially cause serious or even permanent damage. For the current to be safely restored, the short must be identified and carefully repaired.

Love is a lot like electricity, not only in how it serves us but also in how we take it for granted.

Most people move through life expecting to love and be loved. However, our actual experiences can fall short, causing disruptions in the current of love. Just like a short circuit creates a barrier that keeps electricity from flowing properly, over time barriers to love can form too. These barriers keep us from shaping culture with the kind of love that creates change. They also short-circuit our ability to fully experience the power of love available to us through our sphere of influence.

Identifying and understanding the impact of these barriers, or short circuits, is key to developing and keeping a healthy current of love functioning in your life. It only takes a little honest self-reflection to discover where you need to grow in order to love better.

You may not like to hear this, but your inability to love well is a deficiency in your character. Relax—we all have character deficiencies. They present opportunities for us to grow, and it's the training ground where we learn to love.

Learning to love is not a natural process. You may think you know how to love well, but most people don't. We've been led astray by cultural definitions and barriers that create obstacles to becoming a truly loving person. But you can learn to love well if you're willing to put in the effort.

So, what prevents you from loving?

On the circuit board below, draw breaks on the lines between things that keep you from loving fully. Feel free to write your own in the blank spaces.

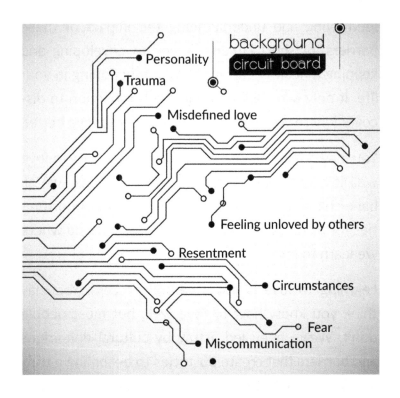

Keep these things in mind as you read the next section. Identifying the barriers is the first step to becoming a more loving person. If you dedicate yourself to identifying and repairing your short circuits, you'll be surprised to find how drastically it can help you overcome fear with love.

Identify Your Barriers

Not all barriers are bad.

They can help us avoid possible danger in life. Just like temporary road barriers direct traffic safely during the construction process, our barriers to love can likewise provide us direction for growth. Learning how barriers affect people can help you understand the challenges we all face in becoming more loving and can assist you with overcoming your own.

Stop for a moment now and look internally. Where do you struggle with love? And why?

Trauma and Woundedness

Trauma, emotional wounds, and brokenness have a significant impact on relationships. Everyone has trauma—it's an inevitable part of being human and living in a chaotic world. But the effects of trauma come in many different forms. Someone who is deeply wounded might respond by being overly controlling, cautious, or angry. Barriers formed by traumatic events and woundedness may even cause a mental health struggle. These complications make it harder to love yourself and others. They also make it challenging to recognize and accept love from others.

Understanding our fears can help point us toward the traumas and wounds that are still creating barriers to love in our lives. While they are not simple to overcome, recognizing them and how they are impacting us will establish a starting point for developing a greater sense of freedom. As we grow, our ability to begin extending love increases when we take steps to heal.

Incomplete View of Love

If you've bought into a cultural definition of love, you may have difficulty recognizing and expressing real love. This is a sign that your view of love is incomplete. You may be trying to fulfill your need for love with something that falls short of all the potential that love has to address every situation and all dimensions of your life.

Perhaps you've never experienced restoration because you think conflict is the end of every relationship. Whenever your relationship with someone has become difficult, you think it's over. If they hurt you, you may be unwilling to forgive without conditions attached to that forgiveness. This kind of perspective dramatically limits love because it only includes outcomes that you perceive as satisfactory.

Another reason for why your view of love may be incomplete is because it's self-defined. Placing yourself as the final authority on love introduces a self-serving dynamic to your life that clouds your ability to receive helpful input from outside sources. It also makes it extremely difficult to communicate with others because there is no shared language or common agreement about what love is. In turn, this just creates more fear by leaving people wondering if they will ever authentically experience love.

In order to overcome this barrier, you need to be willing to rethink your definition of love. Be willing to acknowledge that it's much greater than what you have thought and be open to embracing a view of love that's much bigger than you. When you do, it can function as a catalyst for change in your life in a way you've never envisioned.

Lack of Experience

Maybe you've experienced very little love in your life. If you grew up in a home that didn't value love, especially if you didn't receive love from your parents, you may not know what it's like to love and be loved. It's very possible that this barrier may overlap with trauma. For example, if you've experienced betrayal, it can make it tremendously difficult to trust others. When the people in your life who were meant to love you most didn't meet your needs, the damage can be extensive.

Parental love in the early stages of life is essential for forming our overall view of love. Without it, a person can feel lost and left searching to fill their need for love. If the people who were supposed to love you didn't, it's difficult to know what love is supposed to look like.

If that's you, take a moment and imagine—what if there is someone who loves you? What if you've been loved your whole life and you didn't know it? Would that change how you live?

You cannot allow a lack of love in your past to keep you from experiencing love fully in the future. By extending love to others, even if it feels unnatural, you will increase the potential to receive love in return. You must be willing to risk it, even if it means going first.

Personality Traits

Have you really noticed just how different others are from you?

The variety and uniqueness found in every individual is a beautiful reality of life. But it can also be a source of great frustration if we allow our differences in personality to dominate or dictate the exchange of love.

Differences in personality are not good or bad, but we can often make them the reason for withholding love from another person. Many marriages end for this very reason, but they don't have to. Our personalities are not permission to be unloving. Instead, they are one of the greatest opportunities we have to establish love in a relationship.

Some people think, "I'm just not a loving person," or "I'm fundamentally damaged and not capable of loving well." They use their personality as an excuse to not try.

Some people live life from a place of resignation, believing, "It's just the way I am." But this is simply not true! Anyone can become more loving.

One of the most tangible forms of transformation available to every person is the potential to love in more significant ways. It may not be easy, but it is possible. It's also something everyone can do regardless of how they are wired.

Our personalities also affect the way we interact with love. You may hunger for love in very specific ways and not feel that you're receiving quite what you want. This is because your personality affects the way you interpret and recognize love.

Many of our problems in love can be traced back to personality traits we must wrestle with as barriers. Personality assessments can be extremely helpful for providing insight into your personality. The Five-Factor Model in psychology is widely regarded as the gold standard for personality assessment and is a great way to get started. If you're serious about limiting the impact of your personality on your relationships, take the time to complete some assessments and read about your own personality.

If you don't believe in personality tests, ask your trusted friends and family members to give you helpful feedback about your personality. Here are a few good questions to ask:

- What is something you appreciate about me?

- If you could change something about me, what would it be?

- How do you experience me?

One caution with this approach is to make sure that those you invite into the process of giving feedback are trustworthy and have your best interest at heart.

Resentment

Harboring resentment is another common barrier that keeps people from fully experiencing love. Transformational love *is* forgiving, and you cannot experience the change you desire until you learn to release resentment through forgiveness. It has been said that harboring resentment and refusing to forgive is like drinking poison and expecting the other person to die. Holding a grudge does more harm to you than to the person you're angry with.

When we extend love to others, there is always the chance that we will get hurt. Some relationships won't work out. And we have to move on from those rather than allowing those wounds to become infected and stay with us for life. Forgiveness is the key for processing resentment.

The truth about love is that it cannot be forced. You can't make somebody love you. Not every relationship you have will provide you with fulfilling love, and that's okay. You can continue to extend love to everyone around you, knowing you will receive love back from some of your relationships and that love will be stronger than what you could have received from someone who does not want to love.

Circumstances

It's easy to blame a lack of love on your circumstances. "Look how terrible life is for me."

If you think the world owes you something, you're never going to get what you truly need. Your circumstances are never an excuse.

None of us can control the lot we're cast, and it may be truly an unfortunate situation, but that doesn't mean you're incapable of love. In fact, love is the only thing that will satisfy you regardless of your circumstances. Love also has a radical way of changing circumstances that may not otherwise change.

Miscommunication

Sometimes when you don't *feel* loved, it's easy to think someone doesn't love you. It's possible that they simply may not have communicated it in the way you need to hear it. It can go the other way around, too—sometimes someone doesn't extend love because they don't feel love from you, and that is because you're not communicating in a way that translates to them.

You've likely heard of *The Five Love Languages*, the popular book by Gary Chapman. The principle behind it is that people give and receive love in certain ways. They express their love in the way that makes the most sense to them and feel most loved when they receive it in that way. If we don't communicate these needs to each other, it may not feel like there's much love in our relationships.

In general, it's not common for people to take the time to learn each other's love languages. While it's become a more popular subject and is a common tool for couples to use, how often do we extend those lessons beyond our romantic relationships and immediate family?

If someone gives you a gift, don't reject it—that might be their love language even if it's not yours. By accepting love, you are extending love to others. There is more joy in loving than receiving love, and you give others that joy by graciously accepting their love.

The Five Love Languages proves the point that you have been loved deeply whether you feel it or not. It's likely there are many people in your life who love you more than you know, but you don't recognize it because they're not speaking your love language.

We're all different people. Love looks at someone else and asks, "What can I do to love that person well in our differences?"

Loving well means putting in the effort to understand others, and it begins with communication.

Fear

You probably have a pretty good understanding of how fear functions by now. In a way, it encompasses many of the other barriers to love. We're afraid to act differently and to change our lives, so we don't try to push past our barriers.

But fear can also affect your ability to love more directly. If you're afraid of getting hurt by others, you may sabotage your relationships before someone is able to get close enough to potentially hurt you. Newsflash—you're going to get hurt in relationships. There is no such thing as a relationship that doesn't have conflict. But love will help you get through the conflict and allow you to grow from it.

Growth is hard. It can be painful. And getting over your fears can be one of the most difficult areas to grow. Just remember that nothing good is going to happen until you extend yourself in love.

Fix the Broken Circuit

Take a look at yourself. It's time to self-diagnose. Do you feel alone? Why? Chances are a circuit breaker may have tripped in your life, or something else is causing a dangerous interruption in the current of love.

This step is critical because overcoming your barriers is essential to fully experience love.

If you feel alone and you don't make these changes, you will always be alone. Your life will never get better until you overcome whatever is tripping your circuit.

Stop for a moment and imagine your life. What would happen if you began to extend love to the people around you? How quickly would your life improve?

Imagine. Think with us. What would life be like if, rather than sitting at home or waiting for things to happen in your daily life, you volunteered somewhere?

What if you called up an old friend?

What if you responded to your kids with patience instead of irritability?

What if you sought to make kindness a central part of your character?

Your life is never going to change unless you take action and initiate the gift of going first. That's how it works. You have to give love to get love. It has to start with somebody. If there's no love in your life, you have to go first!

Break Your Barriers

What are your barriers to love?

It's possible that one or more of the barriers to love listed below are creating challenges for you. We have provided space for you to explore ways you can begin confronting this barrier in your life.

- Trauma or woundedness keeps you from loving well.

- You have an incomplete view of love and have been searching for the wrong kind of love.

- You lack experience in love and aren't sure how to do it well.

- You have personality traits that keep you from loving well.

- You harbor resentment or bitterness.

- Your personal circumstances get in the way of loving well.

- You don't know how to communicate love, or others don't communicate their love for you well.

- You're afraid of getting hurt and avoid loving others.

Do you know anyone with one of these barriers to love? What are steps you can take to begin loving them well?

"Love is an endless act of forgiveness."

—Beyoncé

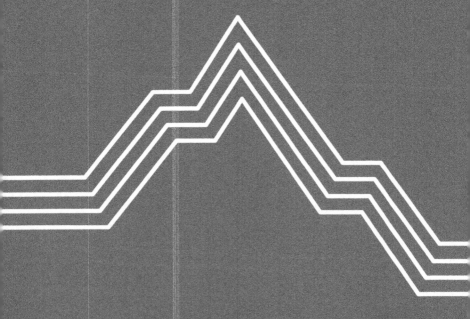

DAY
11

Create Space to Heal

Healing is not easy. And it isn't simple either.

All of us have been wounded by life, causing broken-ness and leaving scars. And if we don't understand the process for identifying how we've been injured, treating these issues properly can become incredibly frustrating.

Healing is not an instant process. Sometimes, it can take years. So, having the right perspective on the healing process is essential. It's important to know that the road to healing is not a sprint but a marathon—one that produces a deep sense of fulfillment as we make progress toward wholeness. Our culture conditions us to value instant gratification, especially in the face of pain. Normally, this results in various forms of coping that often only compound the problem. Proper healing moves *through* the pain over time rather than finding ways to avoid it.

Identifying your wounds and barriers to love is a great place to start. Maybe something stood out to you on the list of barriers to love. If not, continue your diagnostic examination.

How do you identify places where you're broken or wounded? Much like a physical wound, we can tell where we're hurt by the presence of pain. Where is your pain? You can analyze your pain on three levels: physical, emotional, and spiritual.

Start with the physical level. Take an inventory of your body. We sometimes forget that we feel our emotions physically. Where do you feel discomfort, pain, or pressure? Is it an ache in your head, or a nauseous feeling in your gut, or a tightness in your chest? Are you holding tension in your shoulders or jaw?

The physical pain can also help you discover the linked emotional pain point. Of course, we don't experience emotional pain in the same way we do physical pain. But similar to your body, you may feel the pain more acutely when you exercise that part of you. Maybe your knee only hurts when you bend your leg—that tells you something is likely going on inside the joint. Similarly, if you feel pain in association with a certain memory, that could be a trauma that you need to work through. Or if you feel pain in particular situations, that tells you there's an associated emotional wound there.

- What causes that painful emotion? Is it a failure that hurts the most? Is it betrayal?

- If you feel fear in a particular scenario, what is the root of that fear? If you feel pain when trying to make friends or connect with people on a deeper level, why is that?

- What kind of pain is it, and how much pain do you feel?

- Is it acute (temporary) or chronic (long-lasting)?

There's a third level of pain that's even harder to put a finger on—we'll call it spiritual pain. This is something deeper than the emotions you feel in your body. It could be a deep sense of loss, purposelessness, lack of meaning, or lack of value. Perhaps something about you doesn't feel whole. These deeply rooted wounds can be some of the most difficult to heal.

Identifying your wounds, where you hurt, and your pain threshold is a process that could take years, and it happens simultaneously as you grow to understand transformational love. It's a big part of how we develop into more mature and loving people. Depending on how self-aware you are, your healing process could continue for the rest of your life.

But as you heal, you will begin to feel more stable and settled as the pain dampens, even if you're healing slowly. It is worth the effort no matter how difficult it is or how long it takes.

Your internal injuries aren't visible. If people can see you walking around on a broken leg, they can have sympathy and they can express it. But most people are carrying wounds on the inside. Relationships are vital to the process of healing. Share your wounds and involve other people; it allows them to give you love and gives them an opportunity to share their own wounds so you can express love in return.

Why and What?

Love is intentional.

For us to experience the kind of love that transforms, we must account for all the aspects involved in loving. It starts with *thinking* and understanding why you think the way you do.

As you've gone through this book, you've been re-thinking what you believe about love. We hope you've embraced the new view of transformational love, and now it's time to take it one step further.

Remember the Greek word *metanoia*, which means a profound change of heart. How does one actually see this kind of change take place? It begins by thinking about your thinking.

"Why?" is the first question to ask as you begin exploring how your thought patterns formed in the first place.

You can apply this concept to anything in your life. If you want to change something about yourself, it begins with understanding why you haven't done so already or why you may be avoiding it.

It's by asking "why" that you identify faulty patterns of thinking, which have been conditioning your actions.

You've heard it said that even if you don't feel like it, start doing it, and then you'll feel like it. Have you actually tried this? Did it work? For many people, it doesn't. The reason is because the lack of action is driven by a belief. And that belief must change for anything to be different. A new pattern of thinking must replace the old one.

This is where the question "why" becomes the catalyst for change. Want to become more fit? Some would say to start exercising, even if you don't feel like it. And after you've started, it will get easier. If this was actually the case, there would be no unused gym memberships, and everyone would fulfill their New Year's resolutions. If you want to be in better shape, then ask yourself why you don't exercise. What is it that keeps you from making or maintaining changes?

The same goes for reading more books, cooking healthier meals, spending more time with your family, starting your own business, or any other area you want to grow.

Once the reason why is identified, your mind needs to experience a new response to begin breaking a recurring pattern.

Apply that to love. There are reasons why it can be so difficult to begin loving in certain situations. Sometimes these can be challenging to identify, but when you do, significant and lasting change is possible.

"Why?" is a question of the mind. It provides valuable information and insight into whatever challenge you are facing. But just understanding why you do or don't do something will not change it. You have to ask a heart question—a question of desire.

This is where you must ask a follow-up question—the "what" question. Once you have identified the "why," you then need to decide *what* you are going to do about your new insight. Do you actually want it to change? This moves you from evaluation in the mind to reflection in your heart. Your will is made up of both the mind and heart, and when you engage them both, your actions will follow.

Are you familiar with neuroplasticity? The neuropathways in our brains can actually change. You can change the way you think and the way you behave. Science shows us that you really can teach an old dog new tricks, and the brain is more malleable than we used to think. We are more capable of change than we realize. If you are willing to put in some effort to retrain your brain, new ways of thinking can be created.

So how do you reprogram your brain?

There are three conditions for neuroplasticity: the knowledge must be useful, you must have aerobic activity, and the change has to occur over a long period of time.

What does that look like as you begin to think about your thinking?

First, change how you think about love. Question and expand your view of love and consider that love that is bigger and more powerful than you've realized.

Next, take a walk and think about love at the same time. Start adding in information about love as you move your body. Listen to an audiobook about it or a great podcast while you are walking, and make it your focus as you move.

Do this continually, and you will reprogram your brain to become more loving over time.

If you're interested in learning more about neuroplasticity, check out Curt Thompson at https://www.youtube.com/watch?v=dBBsNoC1D50.

Go First

Love inspires love—that's part of what makes it so transformational.

As you grow to become more loving, you can't just sit around waiting to receive love. You have to be willing to go first. That means resolving to love someone whether they love you back or not.

That's the nature of love. It's a driving force that comes out of us like a fountain and spills onto others. We have to be willing to let that drive us. We must learn to love in a way that gives and requires nothing in return.

You want to be happy? Learn how to give yourself away. Learn how to love.

Here is a list of small ways that we can show others love. Go first. Choose three to do today.

- Instead of speeding up in your commute, slow down and let someone merge.

- Hold the door for an approaching stranger whether they say thank you or not.

- Smile and say hello to a stranger on the street or a neighbor you haven't met.

- Offer to handle the dishes, the cooking, or another chore for a family member.

- Intentionally celebrate the success of another person at school or work.

- Put down your phone for a few minutes and listen to someone talk about their day.

- Support a just cause either financially or with your time.

- In a conversation, ask another person two intentional questions about them.

- Take someone else's grocery cart back to the cart return.

- Write an appreciation note to a friend.

- Take a co-worker's shift or stay late at work to help someone with their workload.

- Offer to watch the children for some parents who could use a break.

Forgive

As you become more loving, inevitably you'll be challenged to love people you don't like, but what about people who've wronged you?

You can't be a truly loving person while harboring hatred or resentment. Not only do these things keep you from fully extending love, but they are also harmful to you as untreated wounds. Forgiveness allows those wounds to heal.

Forgiveness isn't easy to do and there is no sign at the end of the road telling you when you've actually forgiven someone.

Let's look at what forgiveness is so you can identify when you've experienced it.

There are two forms of forgiveness. The first form is to pardon or forgive a debt. This is a formal kind of forgiveness, because in order for you to pardon someone, there must be an admission of guilt. Therefore, it's conditional. If someone knows they wronged you and they admit to it, you are able to forgive them that debt.

The second type of forgiveness is nonconditional, and this type is often more difficult to do. It is to give grace and to extend love. Both parties don't have to be present in order for the forgiveness to happen. This is also a more powerful form of forgiveness because it allows you to let go of old wrongs and heal your wounds without an admission of guilt. The person who hurt you doesn't have to apologize or even realize they made a mistake. You are able to be free by simply overlooking the offense.

Because forgiveness can be difficult to do, how do you know if you've really forgiven someone?

If you believe someone owes you something—an apology, an emotional debt, or something else—you haven't forgiven them. Forgiveness is no longer holding that debt over their head, whether they know it or not. When you've forgiven someone, there is no longer a requirement for repayment.

You can tell if you've done this by examining how you feel. The indicator of real forgiveness is freedom.

Do you feel free? Or are you still carrying resentment or hurt?

Forgiveness doesn't always mean reconciliation or restoration of a relationship. It's more powerful than that because it puts the power in *your* hands, not the hands of the one who hurt you. But it does mean that when you forgive, you're able to let go of your wounds and be free of the anger and pain that resentment was causing you. It is an act of love toward others and yourself.

Forgiveness doesn't necessarily happen instantly. It takes practice. You may have to work through your emotional wounds—stitch them up—before you're ready to forgive someone fully. But there is no wrong-doing that can't be forgiven.

Victor Frankl was a Holocaust survivor. After he survived the atrocities of a concentration camp, he wrote, "Everything can be taken from a man but one thing: the last of the human freedoms—to choose one's attitude in any given set of circumstances, to choose one's own way."

We know freedom has been achieved when we're able to move on. We are often imprisoned by our traumas because we've been unable to forgive.

Whatever has happened in your past, you're capable of forgiving. It may hurt to even think of forgiving, and it may take some emotional labor to do it, but once you have given grace and extended love, you can be free.

Forgiving someone in this way does not mean you thought what they did was right. You're not pardoning their wrongdoings. That's for that person to deal with. But in forgiving them, you're choosing to move on and not look at those offenses anymore.

Examine Others' Intentions

It's much easier to forgive someone whom you believe has your best interest at heart. What do you do when someone who loves you does something to hurt you?

Step back and examine the situation. Was the hurt intentional? Did it come from a place of love, of oversight, or of malice? In most cases, they probably weren't doing it out of malice.

People can hurt you with a number of intentions. Sometimes a friend does something that hurts your feelings, and they aren't even aware their actions hurt you. You may perceive their intentions as negative even when they were not. Take a step back and consider whether this person loves you. No one who truly loves you would intend to harm you. Even in a lapse of selfishness, someone who truly loves you will seek to heal the relationship and apologize when they realize they hurt you.

The problem arises when hurt is not communicated. How is someone supposed to know they've hurt you if you don't tell them? It's easy to hurt someone on accident. Everyone does it. You've done it, whether you realize it or not.

You cannot hold people accountable for things they don't know they've done. But a lot of people stay in that place of resentment, holding on to grudges and never communicating when they've been hurt. It may be fear that keeps them from expressing how they've been hurt. We've been sitting on our hurt feelings, blaming someone for a misdeed, because we never communicated with that person and gave them a chance to apologize.

We gain freedom from resentment through forgiveness, but we also gain freedom from fear through our ability to share our wounds and tell people when they've hurt us.

If you're going to tell someone they've hurt you, you must go in with the right attitude. You can't have expectations or requirements—you must be okay with the fact that they may not respond well. There is risk involved, but also potential benefit if you can strengthen your relationship with that person.

On the flip side, consider the people you may have hurt even if it wasn't your intent. You have an opportunity to restore those relationships and extend love to those people by reaching out to them to apologize.

Recognize the Hard Truth

While we've all been hurt by people unintentionally, it's also possible that you've been hurt by someone's actions or words when they were genuinely trying to help you. To love someone is to know, want, and do what's in their best interest. This can be tricky, because it's often difficult to know what's in someone's best interest. And it tends to be even trickier for us to know what's in our *own* best interest.

The truth is, if you truly love someone, you're willing to do something they don't like—maybe even hurt their feelings—because it's in their best interest. This could take the form of telling someone the truth about their negative behavior. They may take offense and believe that you've hurt them when you were only trying to help them.

A more serious example is giving help to an addict. They may not want help. They may fight you. But you know that continuing to feed their addiction is not in their best interest. And while keeping them from whatever they're addicted to may be painful in the short term, ultimately, you're doing it for their good.

There are many times throughout life when we must inflict some discomfort or pain on someone we love for their own sake. As a parent, you may have to keep your child from doing something they want to do that you know is dangerous, or you may have to make them do something they don't want to do or are afraid of, such as going to the doctor or completing their homework.

As a friend, you may have to keep another friend from driving when drunk. Chances are, at some point in your life, you will have to tell someone something they don't want to hear, but you know they need to hear it. It might hurt, but ultimately, it will be for their benefit.

When someone hurts you in this way, it can be easy to become resentful, thinking they don't know what's in your best interest. And perhaps they don't. But if they acted out of love, you know their intentions were not to harm you.

By blaming people blindly without taking the time to examine intentions, you're limiting your relationships. The people who care about you are willing to hurt you because they love you. But if you view yourself as a victim, you'll confuse people's loving intentions as harmful when they're trying to tell you the truth or help you. If they truly love you, they'll be waiting for you when you're ready to accept their love.

Experiencing Freedom

It's time to reflect on your past hurts, losses, and betrayals so you can experience freedom from those wounds and from any resentment.

This process can be painful. Touching old wounds may make them hurt again. Go at your own pace and process one thing at a time.

Who has hurt you in the past?

Write their name here: _____

What was the offense?

Now it's time to leverage the questions *why* and *what*.

Why do you continue to hold on to this offense?

What do you want to do with your pain or resentment? Do you actually want it to change?

The type of freedom we are referring to in this exercise comes through an act of release. Just like handcuffs are removed from a prisoner, experiencing freedom happens when you are released from pain or resentment. When you understand why you hold on to an offense and decide you want to be released from it, freedom can be realized. This process often takes time. You may have to spend some time processing the questions above several times before you can identify what's at the root of lingering pain before it can be released.

"You always gain by giving love."

—**Reese Witherspoon**

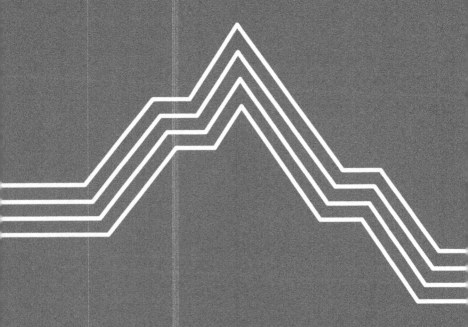

DAY
12

Lose the Loneliness

Have you ever felt alone in a room full of people?

What made you feel that way? What kept you from engaging with others?

What were you afraid of? Rejection? Embarrassment?

Here's something you should know: Everyone battles insecurity.

If we could truly see the thoughts of others in a crowded room, we'd be shocked by the struggle.

We're all wired the same way. Everybody desires connection with others, to have real relationships, to have even just one or two very close friends. But so many people don't. That's why we're succumbing to our fears.

Who do you know that seems to have it all together and has plenty of connected relationships? How did you develop that perception of them? Does the person post frequently on social media? Are they always talking with people? Whatever it is, they're looking for love just like you are.

Think about the social interactions at a junior high dance—everyone wants to dance, but nobody's going to ask. How often do we run into the same kind of situation even as adults? Everyone wants the same thing, but nobody's willing to ask. We find it too difficult to talk to strangers even in the same room.

If you want to come out of the dark and experience connection, then you need to initiate. You have to reach out and become vulnerable.

If you want to have a friend, you have to first be a friend.

If you never want to feel alone again, plug into the circuitry of love. If you're a loving person, you'll draw other people to you. Just like electricity, electrons are drawn together into a flow, and it keeps the lights on. And as long as the lights are on, there's no darkness. As long as you're connected to the ultimate source of power, there is nothing to fear.

Reconnect

Love displaces fear like light displaces darkness. It doesn't have to fight it—all it has to do is touch it. As we expose more parts of our lives to love, our fears fade like darkness fades in the presence of light.

By loving others, we expand the amount of light in our lives. We're plugging in to a larger source—one that allows us to give and receive love so we can experience it more fully.

Fear loses its power in the presence of love. It takes just a little bit of light in a dark room to be able to see everything, and suddenly everything doesn't seem to be so scary. In the same way, the light that love gives us allows us to understand our surroundings better so we can discern who to trust and what to do.

We need each other. Humans are social creatures who depend on each other for survival. In fact, it is through these relationships that we find our satisfaction in life.

According to anthropologist Margaret Mead, the first sign of civilization in a historical human culture is a healed femur that had been broken. Why? Because a human cannot survive a broken leg alone. For a femur to heal, someone must care for that person.

In exactly the same way, we need each other emotionally. We can't heal by ourselves, and we heal faster with each other. We become less afraid of getting hurt when we have others we can depend on who truly know, want, and do what's in our best interest.

Isolation is one of the core fears because isolation can kill us. We cannot live alone. We can be alone for periods of time, but we cannot live that way continuously. If isolation does not physically kill us, it will destroy us in other ways. It will eventually diminish and even disintegrate our souls.

So many of us are living alone, even when we're surrounded by people. We have to come out of hiding and build relationships with others. We have to reconnect to the power that only love can supply.

Unify

People's differences are responsible for a lot of conflict and misunderstanding in this world. And we use them as an excuse not to connect with one another. That's why we have cliques and groups of similar people who spend time together.

Ultimately, it creates disconnection. We all want and need the same things, but somehow we find it very difficult to love each other with our differences.

You may be willing to become a more loving person, but are you willing to love someone you don't like? Are you willing to love a group of people you disagree with?

We're asking you to be different.

Don't try to settle your differences. We're calling you to embrace different personalities, experiences, and backgrounds. Relationships with people who are unlike you are necessary for growth. Even the people you think the least of have something to teach you, whether you believe they do or not.

We tend to live within our own little tribes, but when we've exhausted those social circles and their ideas, we feel empty.

Real love brings unity. We have faults and differences, but we're wired in different ways that allow us to accomplish things when we come together and recognize each other's uniqueness.

What does unity look like? It's not the same thing as diversity. Everyone seems to want diversity, but what we really need is unity *in* our diversity.

Diversity emphasizes our differences, while unity emphasizes our similarities. But unity doesn't require uniformity. It doesn't demand that we all agree. It doesn't demand that we all look, act, and talk the same.

Unity is not unity if it just includes people who look, act, and sound like you.

But it does demand that we have a common human experience and a common commitment to love.

We know that love is discerning without being discriminatory. Seeing our differences doesn't mean changing the differences—it means finding the commonality.

And what we have most in common is that we all want to love and be loved.

Are you contributing to unity?

If you truly want to grow as a loving person, love will eventually expose the places where you are not contributing to the common good. It will reveal how your mindset and beliefs divide instead of unite.

Do you want to be connected or disconnected to other people? Would you prefer to have a sense of unity with fellow human beings, or disunity?

We all think unity is a good idea, but in reality we have let our fears drive us apart.

It's time that we begin to move toward others who are not like us—to let love bind us instead of letting fear divide us.

Reach Out

Find someone who is not in your cultural group, some-one totally different than you, culturally, politically, in age, or in income. Ask them these three things:

1. How would you define love?

2. What do you believe is the most powerful force in the world?

3. What does unity look like to you?

"Knowing that we can be loved exactly as we are gives us all the best opportunity for growing into the healthiest of people."

—**Mr. Rogers**

DAY
13

Developing a Healthy View of Self

The *self-help* industry is booming and has now grown to over 13 billion dollars annually. What this tells us is that people are not satisfied with themselves—they wish to change and want to be better but often don't know how to do it.

If self-help was actually working, don't you think the industry would be shrinking rather than growing? Yet it's not. That is because if we want to grow and see significant changes in ourselves, we have to do the opposite of what the self-help movement suggests. We must develop a healthy view of ourselves generated from the *outside*, not inside.

Our true worth and value must be tied to something bigger than ourselves, to a reality much more magnificent than a person could ever define on their own. In a sense, we need to know the grand scheme of things and, more importantly, our place in it.

Some might suggest that this book, *MEGALIFE*, is self-help, but we don't view it that way. What propels a MEGALIFE is help from others, not the kind of help you get in videos, podcasts, or books. It's help that only comes in the form of transformational love.

Your view of self will not become balanced and healthy until you shift your focus off of yourself and onto others. This is where you discover your true value and worth to your family, friends, co-workers, and community.

When you are connected to others in healthy relationships, your value and worth is reflected back to you as people experience you.

You've probably heard countless times that before you can really love others you have to love yourself. However, this phrase is misleading.

The key to loving yourself comes through learning to love others.

What if we don't need to learn to love ourselves more? Or, what if we need to learn to love ourselves differently? Here's the honest truth—we all love ourselves. We're consumed with ourselves and focused on ourselves in some very unhealthy ways. We tend to think about ourselves more than anything else, and we're encouraged to do so by a culture of radical individualism.

Have you ever thought about how many people you would be surrounded by if you were wildly successful at individualism?

The answer is zero! You would be alone. This is because a life driven toward individualism uses others purely as utlity.

A healthy view of self looks beyond your own interests and embraces the interests of others and the common good, knowing that you have something valuable to contribute.

Our natural instinct of self-preservation is part of why we're so afraid. We're constantly fixated on what might happen to us, our dreams, our desires—our lives. It's an overemphasis on the self.

The concept of loving yourself is so popular that a simple Google search generates 2.4 billion results. You will find everything from dedicated websites to targeted TED Talks and formulas from self-professed life coaches. With that many options available, how would you ever know if you were even doing it right?

The self-esteem movement was the gateway to the growing conversation about self-love, but with all the chatter, a clear process that leads to a healthy view of self has become all the more challenging to identify.

A healthy view of self is not about self-esteem or feeling good about your image. It's not about keeping your house clean, eating healthy, and generally treating yourself right. Those things are good, but they have little to do with how we actually love ourselves.

So, how do you love yourself well?

It begins with understanding that worth is something that is assigned to you; it's not defined by you.

When we give ourselves away, we learn from others what makes us worthy of love, and you cannot learn this any other way.

One of the greatest opportunities to give yourself away is by helping others recognize why they are valuable and worthy of love. In a world consumed with the concept of self, this approach will stop people in their tracks and shift the culture of any person, organization, or community. But, it requires you to shift your thinking off of yourself and onto the well-being of others.

A healthy view of self is rooted in the understanding of human value, and by helping others understand what makes them loveable, you discover the same truths about yourself.

You are worthy of love simply because you are human.

There's nothing you need to do to earn it.

Love is a *right*.

But ask yourself this hard question: do you manipulate love for your own self-interest? Do you subtly twist the definition of love to accommodate your own lifestyle choices, desires, or what you want to be true? Everyone is worthy of love, but that doesn't give us permission to run over others or undermine the common good in order to get it.

If you do, then the person you end up harming the most is yourself.

A person like this will never truly experience love because their definition is at odds with reality. What they will most likely experience instead is higher levels of anxiety due to the constant uncertainty. As a result, they won't find authentic love; they'll just serve their own self-interest.

We will not see true cultural change until we stop viewing others as obstacles or opportunities for our own agendas and begin seeing them as worthy of love simply because they're human.

Accepting that our humanity is what makes us all worthy of love is the starting point for developing a healthy view of yourself. This is the most important step.

This is the tipping point.

Engage the Tipping Point

Make a list, draw a picture, contemplate, or talk to someone about how your worth has been reflected to you from others. List what you have learned about your strengths and weaknesses. Then, reflect and write about if there are any ways you have used love for your own self-interest.

Embrace Character Structuring

Earlier in the book we talked about the role love plays in creating stable structure in our lives in the same way that steel beams function in a skyscraper. Even though each of those beams is different, they work together to keep the building standing when force is applied or pressure comes against it.

Character structuring operates very much the same way. It is the process of gaining qualities that provide a greater durability for meeting the demands of life. Some of these qualities you may already possess, and others may still need work. But as the structure of your character develops over time, your ability to understand yourself and love well from that place will increase.

People associate a wide array of traits with strong character. However, not all of them are beneficial for loving well. Some can actually drive a person to be more self-centered and push them away from what's in the best interest of those around them.

Below is a list of words that are often considered to be a part of strong character. Highlight, circle or underline the words that you connect to.

- Humility
- Confidence

- Beauty

- Self-improvement

- Perfection

- Kindness

- Talent

- Realism

- Agreeableness

- Safety

- Respect

Are any of the words you identified associated with traits that could create a barrier for loving well? Of course, we all want to feel good about ourselves, and yet simply feeling good about yourself doesn't mean you possess strong character. The critical factor that makes or breaks the process of character structuring is that you *must begin with a right assessment of self*.

You don't benefit from believing false things about yourself. Instead, it actually creates significant barriers to growth. None of us are capable of living up to the ideals we set for ourselves all of the time. If the structure of your character is rooted in anything other than the truth, you will not have the ability to handle the demands of reality.

The self-esteem movement says that you can be whatever you want to be. But have you ever really thought about that statement? Is it true? Have you tried it? You can't just be whatever you want to be. That's a well-intended lie. You can't necessarily be an Olympian or an astronaut just because you want to. But you can develop yourself and grow your character. This process, however, does not begin in any other place than an honest appraisal of who you truly are. You may find this to be incredibly challenging, especially if you *feel* like you're supposed to be something different than you are.

Regardless of any deficiencies you may have in your character, there is one truth that will allow you to always maintain a healthy view of self—your humanity. You are worthy of love, kindness, patience, and forgiveness simply because you are human.

Reject Perfectionism

The self-esteem movement has produced another challenging presumption in society—perfectionism. Mantras like "become the best version of yourself" and similar sentiments can be detrimental to developing a healthy view of self and strong character structure. Think about it. If "becoming the best version of yourself" is the goal, then how do you know that you are the best version of you at any given moment? What indicates that it's happening? That doesn't mean we shouldn't try to improve, but we must do so with a realistic perspective and definable outcomes.

According to the meta-analysis "Perfectionism Is Increasing Over Time" by Hill and Curran, perfectionism has increased from 1989 to 2016 in all categories, with the largest being "socially prescribed perfectionism," which rose 32 percent. It's also the category most associated with mental illness. Hill and Curran call this new kind of perfectionism "hyper-perfectionism."

Perfectionism causes fear because perfection is unattainable—you will inevitably fail. When it's so common to fear failure, you can see why this creates and exacerbates mental health struggles for so many.

We end up believing we're supposed to achieve something that may not be possible. That kind of un-realistic thinking will drive anyone crazy!

For Hill and Curran, hyper-perfectionism is self-oriented, others-defined, and socially prescribed. If you're under the influence of hyper-perfectionism, you're constantly judging yourself based on your own standards (what you've achieved in the past and what you expect to achieve), what you perceive the stan-dards of others to be (what others have achieved and what you believe they expect you to achieve), and cultural expectations.

Measuring up and keeping up is impossible and ex-hausting because it requires you to work in order to be loved. It's something you have to earn.

But, as we have stated previously, love is not earned. It is a right and not a privilege.

Your value, worth, and purpose are not dictated to you by the world.

A healthy view of self, without perfectionism, allows you to view yourself as valuable where you are now and therefore approach continued de-velopment with the right perspective. It gives you freedom to pursue life and your needs in a healthy way because your view is realistic.

In fact, the potential for healthy relationships, a great job, and a meaningful life increases exponentially when the results are based on a realistic view of yourself and the world.

Renowned Canadian psychologist Jordan Peterson states, "The purpose of life, as far as I can tell ... is to find a mode of being that's so meaningful that the fact that life is suffering is no longer relevant."

The brilliance in Peterson's perspective is that it acknowledges what is true—life is hard, but a meaningful existence is possible.

This is a journey, and as you continue to learn how to love yourself appropriately, a healthier view of self will emerge.

If you struggle with perfectionism, overcoming it will take time. Learn to recognize when you're holding yourself to standards created by perfectionistic thinking, and give yourself grace the same way you would give that gift to someone you love. By doing so, you will reject perfection and embrace progress.

Allow Love to Make Life Better

As you grow in your understanding of transformational love, it will impact all areas of your life. You'll find more value in existing relationships, your current job, and even in your preferred future.

You don't find miserable, fear-driven people doing well in any area of life. Fear may drive high performance for a season, but it eventually leads to collapse. People who thrive are content, grateful, secure, and fulfilled. The key to developing this kind of outlook begins by allowing love to permeate all areas of your life.

What do you really want in life? Is it a better job, a different relationship, or a new context?

Write it here:

Whatever your goals are, there is always something deeper behind them—something you are seeking.

Many would say that what we're seeking is success. But what we really long for is contentment, fulfillment, and satisfaction.

In the space below, brainstorm about how transformational love can make what you want a reality.

Sit Down and Think

You just completed an exercise writing about how transformational love can make what you want a reality. Now it's time to sit down and think.

In the cultures of ancient Greece and Rome, philosophers regularly engaged in a practice of setting aside time to think and talk. They even built places for dialogue and discussion of ideas called forums.

How often do you spend time thinking and not doing anything else? Most people aren't accustomed to it, but it's important in order to learn about yourself.

If you don't make space to think about life, others will do your thinking for you. Letting others define your life, your beliefs, and who you are because you don't take time to think is tragic. Independent thought is a skill that is learned and critical for growth. It is essential for creating clarity.

So we're going to do some self-reflection. You need to sit down and think. But before considering the following question, you may need to create some space in your life in order to do it well. Set aside time to think about these questions.

- What are you?

- Where do you get your value?

- Do you believe humans have inherent worth—that we're something more than an advanced animal or evolutionary accident?

Here are your options: you are either an accident or you're not.

What do you believe about the soul? Do you think you have a soul? What you believe about this affects your ability to love in every way because it determines how you view the worth of every human being—including yourself.

If humans don't have souls, then how we treat one another shouldn't really matter. We should instead just accept whatever happens in life as a futile exercise in which only the strongest survive.

Can you see the conflict here?

You may have been taught you're just an advanced animal, but what if you're not? What if you're more, and what if everyone else is too?

Perhaps it's time to consider a different and better narrative.

A Right View of You

What are five traits about you that contribute to your ability to love well?

1.

2.

3.

4.

5.

"To get the full value of joy you must have someone to divide it with."

—**Mark Twain**

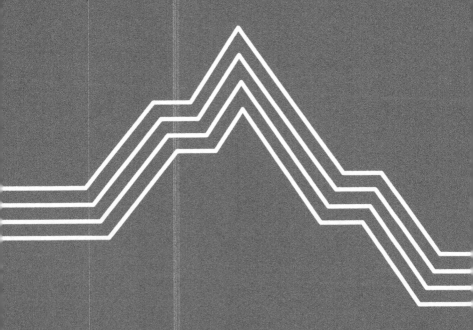

DAY
14

Love as a Way of Life

By now you are probably beginning to appreciate that building a MEGALIFE is both a challenging and rewarding undertaking. It will stretch you well beyond your comfort zone, taking you to a place of deep experimentation and self-discovery that cannot be experienced any other way.

At times, it may become disorienting and even daunting, but this is how old patterns of living are broken and new patterns are formed.

If you want love to be a way of life for you, it will only happen through something called integration.

Integration is the process by which what we believe or desire becomes realized in everyday living. It's how change establishes new patterns of behavior, which creates new habits and ultimately forms character.

A helpful way of viewing integration is looking at it like a bridge you must cross. If you don't take the first step, then you'll never see what's on the other side. However, some bridges feel strong and sturdy while others feel unsteady and perilous, like a rope bridge stretched across a canyon.

Expanding your view of love and integrating it into all dimensions of life will at times feel like both. As you grow and develop, stability will come as your experience yields the kind of change you only thought was possible. But there will also be times when you're hanging on and wanting to give up.

But don't! Discouragement is the evidence that integration is happening.

As you begin the process of integration, we want to provide you with a helpful framework for growth.

We call it *The Four Dimensions of Human Health.*

Having a structure for the integration process is essential for two reasons: it provides definition and context for categories of growth and also the means to evaluate progress.

The truth about love is that it's functional and structural for all of life. When integrated, it influences your health in every way: emotionally, relationally, intellectually, and vocationally. In time this will equip you with the ability to know, want, and do what's in the best interest of others as well as the common good.

Emotional Health

Emotional health is developed by learning how to process emotions in a way that fosters growth. As a result, greater emotional stability is added to your character. Areas of focus include fear, vulnerability, desire, and happiness. Trauma is also an important category because of its impact on your ability to be emotionally whole. Therapy, intensive experiences, recovery, and support groups are all tools to consider for growth in this dimension.

Relational Health

Becoming relationally healthy means that you're developing the kind of skills necessary to relate functionally with family, friends, co-workers, and even acquaintances. This includes your ability to communicate, connect, handle conflict, forgive, and build lasting friendships.

Intellectual Health

Being healthy intellectually is directly connected to how you view the world—your ability to think independently about life. It starts with having an accurate and balanced view of reality. A healthy worldview helps us deal with the demands of reality and guards against unreasonable expectations and unhealthy agendas. As your intellectual health matures, it is one of the most significant tools for combating fear and anxiety as your experience and reality begin to align.

Vocational Health

Vocational health is about action. It's learning to exercise your power and influence in a healthy way. As you grow in this dimension, you take more ownership of your strengths, weaknesses, talents, skills, and personality. This is where what the world needs and what you are made to do converge. Assessments, coaching, and leadership development cohorts are great resources for becoming healthy vocationally.

Love as a way of life is not blind love—it is purposeful love. We encourage you to be thoughtful about how you apply it as you begin integrating it into all the dimensions of your life.

Transformational love does not congratulate a fool as they jump off a cliff. Instead, it says "Don't jump!" even if it's unwelcome or unpopular.

Transformational love is also protective. It emphasizes the well-being of others by helping them see what is in their best interest, even though it could be painful or costly for you both.

There are also healthy limitations for integrating love as a way of life that include making the space and time to care for yourself. We are not suggesting that you love without ever having regard for yourself. When we don't take care of ourselves with proper rest, diet, exercise, and recreation, we undermine our ability to love. The truth is that we love better when we feel better.

In summary, wanting what's in the best interest of others means making calculated choices on the behalf of other people. What's best for them? What's best for you? What's best for your family? What's best for your organization or company? What's best for your community? What's best for your culture?

Love wants what's best not just for individuals, but for everybody.

It's a perspective that considers the whole over self.

It's a way of life.

Extending Love to Others

By integrating love into all dimensions of your life, you will begin to see more opportunities to love others. And when they arise, you will have to decide which opportunities you will step into and which ones you won't.

We only have so much bandwidth in life for relationships, and it can be unloving to create expectations for others that you cannot fulfill. Extending love beyond yourself is an area where we as people will continue to grow throughout our lives, but we must be cautious to not overextend ourselves. As you love more people, you will begin to experience true transformation and the fulfillment that comes with it. You will also learn there is even more joy to be found in loving than in being loved.

Once you've recognized your own inherent dignity and value, you are more prepared to affirm that in others. In fact, you must. You simply cannot appreciate your own value without acknowledging the same about those around you. If your value comes from being human, then every other human has the same value as you.

Throughout this book, we've been challenging you to change how you think about love.

Now it's time to talk about *how* you do it.

So, how do you love others?

It happens with changes in thought, feeling, and action. These three changes must work in concert for love to translate—for the circuit to be complete.

We may know in our minds what we can do to be more loving, and we may also desire to do it in our hearts. But if we don't act, then love will not transfer from us to others.

A subtle shift in your mindset away from how others can serve you to how can you serve others is a great starting point. Choose to put them first. It sounds simple and cliché, but the hard work is making the choice. In turn, this helps others learn about their dignity and shows them why they are worthy of love. In other words, it helps them connect to the right current.

Love inspires love. Choose a life of influence through inspiration by giving rather than taking.

There's a difference between *acts* of service and a *life* of service. Both can be fulfilling, but with acts of service, the fulfillment doesn't last. They may give you an emotional high for the day, but they don't bring deep and lasting fulfillment.

Seek regular opportunities in your life to serve others, to be kind, and to express love. Turn love into a daily commitment and a new way of life.

Love in Action

Finding an Outlet

Did you know you can go to a soup kitchen, slap food on a plate, and still be unloving?

If you're doing it just to make yourself feel good, then you're doing it for the wrong reason. It's not loving when what you're doing is for your own benefit. *Why* you are doing something matters as much as—if not more than—*what* you are doing.

As you seek to find an outlet for putting love into action, know that it will overhaul how you live and act, but most of all, it will overhaul how you think. At times, it will confront what you've come to believe about volunteerism, altruism, and just about every "-ism" there is when it comes to doing good.

There are plenty of service organizations that exist to do good and raise astronomical amounts of money to implement their solutions and feel good about themselves. The problem is that we often see fewer results and limited impact.

Why is that? It's because loving others authentically and actively is not a resource problem—it's a philosophical problem.

It's why we see greed shrouded as a gift in exchange for a tax break or a name on a plaque, and cloaked agendas falsely clothed as justice. Just as love cannot be forced, purchased, or politicized, neither can change. There is no amount of money that can solve systemic cultural issues, and hate will never eliminate hate. That's because the problem runs much deeper in all of us than we realize.

It's embedded in the very fabric of humanity.

In February of 1998 a very surprising speaker took the stage at TED—the late well-known evangelist Billy Graham. Greeted by a standing ovation, the well-known religious figure came to the podium to address the topic of technology and faith. In his talk, Graham stated that in spite of stunning human innovations and countless technological advancements, there are still three problems that we have failed to solve: human evil, human suffering, and death.

Ultimately, Dr. Graham's talk challenged all the great minds in the room with a question that we all must ask ourselves today—how do you solve what seems to be unsolvable?

How do you deal with the fact that regardless of how passionately you may believe in the need for change, there will always be people who won't care? Even more, what do we do about people in the world who are dead set against positive change?

Finding an outlet for love accounts for these realities by seeking to add more love to culture—not less. True change comes at a price higher than money can buy. It comes with sacrifice. It means laying down pride and being willing to consider that maybe, just maybe, *we* are part of the problem.

Love is more than saying the right words or doing good things. It's thoughtfully considering how you can love well by choosing to give yourself away.

Stepping out and finding ways to love others can be difficult. At first, you might wonder where to begin. But as you become more in tune with what's in the best interest of others and the common good, opportunities will emerge.

The goal is to find an outlet connected to the current of love, one that values the dignity of all people, especially when they disagree with you or see things differently.

Let's revisit our definition of love: to know, want, and do what's in the best interest of another person.

How do you determine what's in someone's best interest? And for that matter, who are you to decide what's in the best interest of someone else?

The answer is that if your motivation is to love someone more than you love yourself, it's much easier to have their best interest in mind. Until we're willing to approach relationships this way, none of the most pressing problems in the world are going to change.

Unfortunately, our culture continues to do just the opposite. Everyone has their own agenda and usually fails to recognize how their own path may be hurting others and hindering the common good.

If you really want to be counterculture, consider the ramifications of how you apply your thoughts, desires, and actions to *everyone* around you. It's easy to deny yourself in favor of a family member, your child, or a friend, but it's not as easy to do the same for your neighbor, co-worker, or enemy.

Transformation happens when love turns your thoughts and desires into action.

How Do You Act?

What would life be like if you set out to intentionally act in love? What would happen if you did any of the following? What would it trigger?

- Volunteered your time to serve people who are different than you

- Acknowledged the stranger passing you on the sidewalk

- Listened with patience and compassion to a struggling co-worker

- Re-connected to an old friend you haven't spoken to for a while

- Responded to your family with kindness instead of irritation

Love translates through action. The examples we provided above are just a few examples of what is possible. We encourage you to spend time thinking of some of your own.

Begin with your own home, your school or workplace, and then extend it to your community, and finally greater society.

What can you do to act in love?

Today: _____

Tomorrow: _____

This week: _____

"Love is composed of a single soul inhabiting two bodies."

—**Aristotle**

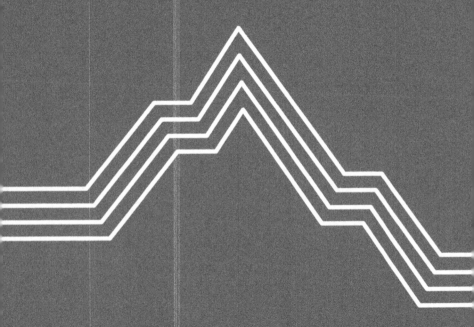

DAY
15

Accepting Love

Throughout this book we have used the analogy of the flow of electricity to describe the exchange of love. We believe this is a valuable illustration because the way electrical currents work mirrors the movement of love from one person to the next in healthy relationships. Just like an electrical current needs an uninterrupted loop or circuit to flow properly, so do relationships. In a healthy relational circuit, love is both given and received.

An electrical circuit is established when a wire is used to create a loop upon which electricity can flow. In a relational circuit love flows from one person to the next through our needs. All of us have needs that are designed to be met in relationship with others. We start learning this during childhood with our parents and then eventually from others as we grow into adulthood.

We call these needs *relational needs* because they are exchanged between two people. Relational needs are important because they foster a healthy emotional climate for mutual lifegiving relationships.

Examples of *relational needs* include the following:

- Security – providing safety even in the face of fear, anxiety, danger, or doubt

- Validation – acknowledging the feelings and ideas of another person as valuable

- Affirmation – stating what is true about another person for their positive benefit

- Acceptance – offering a favorable reception to another person regardless of their flaws

- Support – providing a foundation of patience and stability for another person

- Respect – honoring another person for their dignity as a human being

- Encouragement – inspiring confidence in another person amidst doubt

- Affection – expressing fondness for another person with words or actions

- Comfort – consoling or bringing reassurance to another person in difficult circumstances

A relational circuit that is functioning properly will create and maintain trust, safety, and dependability as needs are recognized and met. But getting our needs met can often seem tricky because of confusion over how the process happens. It's very easy to think that others who love you should automatically know what you need and, in turn, meet those needs.

It would be ideal if this was the case. However, it's unrealistic to think that it's the responsibility of others to meet our needs. What is true is that it's your responsibility to understand what you need and then communicate those needs to others. The hope is that people who have your best interest at heart will hear your request and respond to your needs. Over time, people will become more in tune with one another and meet the expressed needs as an interchange of love.

Learning to accept love is a core element that is essential for building a MEGALIFE. We can all struggle with accepting love for various reasons, but regardless of what stands in the way, it's important for you to evaluate your ability to accept love and the obstacles you might face in doing so. Growth isn't produced only by loving others—you must also learn to be loved.

The Language of Needs

The relational interchange of our needs has a language. Maybe you've never thought about it this way, but without language it's almost impossible to communicate anything. And our needs are no different. When two people begin to use a common needs-based language, two things happen—both parties can identify what is being communicated more easily and the opportunity to love the other person presents itself.

Everyone has needs they don't talk about. Just like wounds, we keep them close, hidden inside us. But it doesn't change the fact that we still expect people to meet those needs without ever having expressed them.

Expressing your needs is an invitation for others to enter into your life. Here's the thing—people are waiting to be invited! But they're not going to insert themselves. We have to allow others into our lives through expressing what we need and asking for their help.

Learning to accept love requires action. It takes initiative and risk, knowing that some people may refuse your request or find themselves incapable of meeting the need. But if you don't even try, you will have a hard time finding anyone who can meet your needs.

You might think that if you wait long enough, someone will show up and just know what you need. But it doesn't work that way. You might be fortunate to find a relationship where needs are met more naturally with less communication. However, this is the exception and not the rule. Using language to describe what we need helps us find people who are capable and willing to respond.

What if you've tried this in the past and it hasn't gone well?

Perhaps you feel that people are not trustworthy because you've been hurt by others who appeared to have your best interest at heart. Risk is a necessary aspect involved in receiving love, and you must avoid the tendency to allow hurt to color all of your relationships.

If you find people who don't respond, then just keep trying with others, because there are people who *will* respond. And you'll never find those people if you stop looking for fear of being hurt.

Meeting needs is the way we deepen the bonds in existing relationships and establish connections with new ones. Opening up to people by expressing your needs is the way to create dependable relationships that will last a lifetime.

Explore Your Needs

Go back to the list of needs earlier in the chapter and choose three that are important to you.

Write out why you believe they are valuable to a relationship and describe what it would be like if they were met to the fullest degree in your life.

Finally, identify three people who you believe could meet these needs in a stable and growing relationship.

Own Your Happiness

In his book *Happiness Is a Serious Problem*, Dennis Prager writes, "We tend to think that we owe it to ourselves to be as happy as we can be. And this is true. But happiness is far more than a personal concern. It is a moral obligation. Upon a moment's reflection, this becomes obvious. We owe it to our husband, or wife, our fellow workers, our children, our friends, indeed to everyone who comes into our lives, to be as happy as we can be."

How is it that Prager can speak about happiness as a moral obligation?

Isn't happiness just a feeling that we can't control?

Happiness is a moral obligation for the same reason we view love as more than just a romantic emotion. Happiness is something that is intentionally built over time by the way a person intentionally designs their life and develops their character.

Happiness is a lifestyle that is directly connected to your view of love. Just as you must take responsibility for becoming a more loving person, you must also take responsibility for cultivating happiness!

Part of maturing is accepting responsibility and taking ownership of how you understand critical aspects of reality such as love and happiness. It's remarkable to see how many people think their happiness is dictated by others, by their circumstances, or by how culture has defined it.

Just as acceptance of love is active, so is bolstering your happiness. If we were honest, we would all admit that we desire to be happy. Connecting to happiness in the heart is easy. However, that's where it tends to end. We long to be happy, but most of us feel that it's up to chance whether we'll experience sustainable happiness in life.

The two most important aspects to forming lasting happiness are thought and action. If we relegate happiness to nothing more than an emotion, like we often do with love, it will remain elusive. But when we work at our happiness with thoughtful intention and corresponding action, the emotions we desire follow.

These emotions can often catch us by surprise as well. They may not show up as the highly charged feelings we generally associate with happiness. Instead, they may arrive in our lives as a subtle, lasting calm and stable sense that every-thing is right and good with life.

Just like with love, we must take a different approach to our understanding of happiness. We need to bring a level of thought and action to the pursuit of a happy life that is worthy of the endeavor. We call this next-level responsibility.

Rather than waiting for others, you must take respon-sibility and ask others to meet your relational needs as a part of building a structured life of happiness.

Why are you leaving your happiness in the hands of other people who don't know what you need to be happy? How do you expect them to know?

Taking responsibility for your own happiness includes knowing how to accept love from others. It's about taking ownership and initiating rather than looking to others for fulfillment and satisfaction. It acknowl-edges the kind of intentional effort that's necessary to produce a life of sustainable happiness.

Next-level responsibility is also about growing your capacity to love.

If you're a parent, your capacity for love grew beyond your spouse when you had your first child. Perhaps you thought you could never love another child as much as you loved the first. But those who have multiple children often express how love develops differently with every child that enters their life.

Love expands.

As your capacity for love grows, so does your responsibility.

Next-level responsibility is when you're responsible not just for yourself, but for others as well. It is about making decisions that are in the best interest of others.

We're challenging you to take ownership of your own happiness not just for yourself but for the benefit of others as well.

Happiness really is a moral obligation.

Reconsider Toxic Relationships

Are you happy with the way people treat you? If not, why do you think they treat you that way? Do you see any patterns? How do you react to their behavior?

We have a say in how we want people to treat us. By continuing to accept mistreatment, we effectively tell them it's okay. Part of accepting love is refusing and pushing back on unhealthy ways of relating. We must refuse to allow it both for ourselves and others.

Many people simply opt out of a relationship when it becomes difficult instead of working on it.

Think back to relationships in your past you no longer have. What caused them to end?

We live in a culture where we quit when relationships become challenging or "cancel" people over differences of opinion.

Staying in difficult relationships takes resolve but can produce great rewards. In order to stay in a relationship with someone who doesn't treat you well, you must set boundaries and refuse to accept their poor behavior. The purpose of boundaries is to establish proper conditions for healthy relationship.

This includes every kind of relationship you have in your life. If you allow your coworkers or your boss to treat you poorly, ultimately, that will result in creating a toxic work situation.

Stating how you desire to be treated and what you need from people is a proactive way to prevent toxic relationships before they start. By doing so, you give others the opportunity to respond by initiating the kind of conversation that produces healthy relationships. People who are loving will respect those boundaries and seek to contribute to the relationship in a positive way.

If you set those parameters and communicate them either verbally or by modeling the behavior and people still do not respect them, you may need to consider cutting ties. However, it's important not to treat ending a relationship flippantly. Toxic relationships always include two participants and can often be a convenient excuse for not wanting to do the hard work that produces a strong relationship.

In *Boundaries for Leaders*, Henry Cloud says, "You create what you allow." If you allow things to continue, then essentially, you're creating that situation. This even extends beyond relationships to how we view problems in life, in our communities, and the culture at large.

Next-level responsibility means you consider the relationships in your life with great care and concern. If you believe a relationship is toxic, you must not just account for how others participate, but how you enter it as well. That is, you must also take responsibility for the role that you play.

Go First

In this chapter, we described a way of thinking about happiness that may be new to you. Use the space below to write about how this will change the way you live. What could you do to take ownership of your own happiness? How can you ask for help in getting your needs met? Where can you go first by extending love to others?

Now, write down three practical steps that will help you begin taking action.

1.

2.

3.

"The best and most beautiful things in the world cannot be seen or even touched. They must be felt with the heart."

—**Helen Keller**

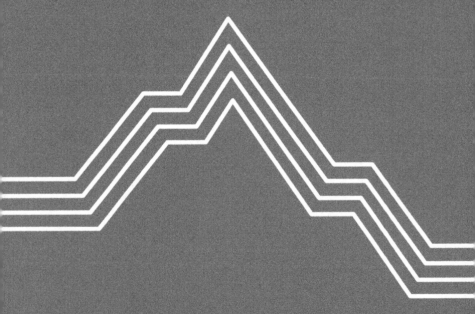

DAY
16

The Box

The purpose of "The Box" exercise is to help you identify the driving philosophy of your life and create meaningful direction for your growth. In the box below, write the answer to the following question with a *single word*:

"What am I trying to become?"

We encourage you to give this a significant amount of thought and choose a word that is substantive enough to carry through all of life—a word that will chart the course for you as you continue to grow.

You can use the area surrounding the box for brainstorming, exploring perspectives that may influence your answer, or creating lists, etc.

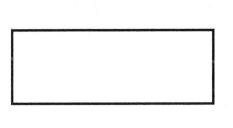

Get Over Yourself

So, how did "The Box" exercise go? Did you find it to be challenging?

Often people find this exercise to be very difficult and even emotional. It forces you to think about the meaning of life—the essence of who you truly are and what you're about.

Did you find yourself avoiding words that seemed shallow?

If so, that's not a surprise.

In his book *Man's Search for Meaning*, Viktor Frankl wrote,

"Don't aim at success. The more you aim at it and make it a target, the more you are going to miss it. For success, like happiness, cannot be pursued; it must ensue, and it only does so as the unintended side effect of one's personal dedication to a cause greater than oneself or as the by-product of one's surrender to a person other than oneself."

As our culture continues to affirm a life of individualism, the message to serve yourself, please yourself, and live only for yourself will only intensify. If Frankl was right, what this means is that people will become increasingly unhappy as they focus on themselves as their source and authority for meaning and happiness.

Are you willing to resist the pressure and surrender to something greater than you?

As we approach the end of this book, we want to be explicitly clear about one thing—living a MEGALIFE means choosing to live for something greater than yourself.

What this really means is that you need to get over yourself!

You might be thinking, "Whoa, that's harsh!" But it's actually the most loving thing we could say. People who focus too much on themselves actually end up feeling isolated and depressed.

So, where do you begin? By simply orienting your life to love well, you are expanding your view beyond yourself. Eventually you will come to realize that this is really just common sense.

Everyone is morally accountable to love well because your actions take a toll on you personally as well as on others. Everything you do affects people around you, the culture, and ultimately the world.

We all have a human responsibility to love others for the common good. Love is how you will find meaning in your life, but it's also how you will do the most good while making your contribution to the world. Will you accept this responsibility?

Connect to the Source

We all have an innate desire to love and to be loved—and through love, to influence culture. We derive our greatest satisfaction through love and relationships and influencing culture in these ways.

Ever wonder where this drive in all of us comes from?

Just like electricity, it has to have a source—something *outside* of ourselves.

All humans have a desire to be part of something greater than ourselves. We're all searching for meaning and purpose in our lives. What is your place in this world? How do you fit? What is your role? What will you contribute, and why does it matter?

When we make the decision to embrace something greater than ourselves, we find fulfillment by actively loving and being loved. We know this to be true, but what most of us are looking for is an anchor. So many people are struggling, grappling for something to hold onto, some kind of truth about life that can guide and ground them. And many things that people try to grab onto are not strong enough to support them. They fail because they aren't anchored well and connected to a sustaining source.

Do you realize that your entire existence is built upon dependence?

As humans, we're dependent on things outside of ourselves to sustain life. You can try to deny it, but you will always be dependent on something greater than you—nature, weather, government, industry, culture, and maybe even your family.

The messages of our world try to convince us that we can be self-sustaining. But this is an outright lie. It tries to convince you that you can make it on your own if you just try hard enough. But what do you do when you've tried as hard as you can and it's not working?

Or what if you've done everything you possibly can and something unexpected ruins your plans? How do you make sense of that?

The source of meaning that is greater than you has to be big enough to make sense of all of life. It has to be able to hold everything in a fine balance that accounts for history, the present, and our future. It must be able to explain suffering, inequality, and even death.

Because we are all at the mercy of these realities.

So, if love is like an electrical circuit, where does the power come from? What is it that you're actually connecting to?

The source is MEGA.

Why is it called MEGA? Because it's so big, and there's so much of it, that it is unquantifiable and unlimited.

Some people try to say that it's the universe. Others think it's a belief in the common good.

We'll call it Something Greater, because it's beyond us all. You don't have to be spiritual to believe in something greater than yourself. But you do need a source, which will power you as you become more loving.

You're at a crossroads, and you have to make a decision. Do you believe there's something higher than you or not?

If you decide that there's not, you must recognize that what you are essentially claiming is that you know enough about everything to determine that there is nothing greater than you. You would have to, therefore, be all-knowing.

Does that sound right? Does that make any sense?

The challenge here is to be open. Would you be open to the idea that maybe there *is* a source greater than you?

What would it take for you to open yourself up to that idea?

Stop and really think. How do you feel when you think about the universe?

Something inside of you probably tells you there has to be more to life. Do you feel a hole, like something is missing? Like life is a puzzle that is missing a piece?

If you do, what if there's something out there that can satisfy that?

We believe love can fill that void, but you have to connect to the ultimate source to fully experience it.

What If 'Why' Is Not the Question?

Simon Sinek in his bestselling book *Start With Why* popularized the importance of asking the question "why?" as the means to self-fulfillment. This single concept has positioned Sinek as a global self-help guru in leadership development circles.

But did you know this idea did not originate with Sinek?

In 1889, Friedrich Nietzsche in his work *Twilight of Idols* stated,

> *"He who has a why to live for can*
> *bear almost any how."*

Nietzsche was also responsible for declaring "God is dead" in his famous work *Parable of a Madman*, authored in 1882. It was his way of stating that the traditional morality of society was meaningless. His ultimate conclusion as a philosopher was that man needed to rise up and become "the Superman"—that mankind could trust his own will, drive, and desire to control a world that was absurd to him.

This kind of thinking can lead to devastating results. If mankind believes he gets to determine his own meaning and has no higher responsibility, it can lead to destructive movements like genocide, slavery, and other horrific events that undermine the value of human life.

Isn't it strange how recycled ideas can cause such horrific devastation?

You can only understand your "why" by first answering the question "who?"

The "who" is critical, because who we trust to inform our "why" can lead to lasting consequences. Who do we allow to determine meaning and purpose in life?

Where does the value that makes something meaningful come from?

Who has ascribed worth to concepts like love and happiness, making them priceless in the eyes of everyone?

If we are unable to identify a source, then everything is truly meaningless. There is nothing higher than ourselves to determine what is meaningful. What we do in this life does not matter. Also, how we treat others is pointless. If you are not able to determine where your desire for a meaningful life comes from, then you're simply playing a mind trick to convince yourself that meaning is worth seeking.

You see, "why" is a question of meaning, but something is only meaningful because it has had value assigned to it by something or someone outside of itself.

We realize that trying to discover the who behind your why can raise a great deal of doubt. So, before we can go any further, we must first deal with that doubt.

Dealing With Doubt

Doubts, like fear, can be a good thing. Doubts lead to questions, which lead to answers. Fear can motivate us to look for answers. Just be honest with your doubts. Ask the questions that lead you to seeking answers. Answers help dispel fear because they give you a solution to the challenge.

What are your doubts?

We have provided space below for you to write out your doubts that may be holding you back.

Now that you've identified your doubts, what questions do your doubts raise?

Do you doubt that there is Something Greater than you?

Do you doubt you have value and worth?

Do you doubt that you will find significant purpose in life?

Write them below:

"Never believe that a few caring people can't change the world. For, indeed, that's all who ever have."

—**Margaret Mead**

DAY
17

True Purpose

True purpose is a key element for building a MEGALIFE, and it can only be found when it's defined by Something Greater. It also connects the dots of truth, meaning, worth, and fulfillment.

Ultimately, it's the greatest way to eliminate our doubts so we can live a fearless life.

When you understand who you are and why you're here, living daily with intention and a deep sense of meaning becomes natural. You can endure anything as long as you have an authentic purpose.

Our culture has significantly undermined the ability to establish a substantial sense of purpose through mantras like "find your passion." This idea has only led to more people trying to find purpose inside themselves, and the concept has become a god for people. What they're really trying to do is fulfill a purpose.

But what if your purpose cannot be found inside of yourself?

If your purpose is outside of yourself, it is more stable. It gives you something to hold onto—a design. So, when fear hits, you have something more solid than yourself to rely on. You become less self-focused and occupied by your fears.

Have you ever seen a ballet dancer perform one pirouette after another without losing their balance? They can do this because they are "spotting," focusing their eyes on a stable spot that grounds them while their bodies are in motion. In the same exact way, when we focus on Something Greater, we don't allow our own emotions or surroundings to disorient us. We can remain stable.

As we move toward the conclusion of this experience, we want you to consider one final question—what if we all have the same purpose?

What if your unique gifts, talents, and personality work to serve a greater purpose that everyone is contributing to?

You can work hard trying to establish your "why," but what happens when your "why" turns out to be worthless? When you've answered all your questions, read all your books, gained success beyond your imagination, and you still haven't found fulfillment—then what?

The subjectivity of everything you've achieved will eventually let you down.

You're chasing something you can never catch. It's eternally evasive, and your definition of success is always being redefined. What do you do after you achieve your dream? You no longer have a purpose, so your purpose must change.

If your purpose or your "why" is self-defined, it is always shifting. Your "why" needs an anchor. It needs a "what": something objective, something central that unites you with those around you. It must be Something Greater than yourself.

Whenever you ask people where society is at today and what needs to change, what do they say? What do we need to make people change and act differently? What would unite people?

"We just need more love."

Everyone knows, deep down, that's the answer.

Love is the "what." And when you understand that, then your "why" changes. It grows beyond yourself.

There is no unity without love. And we need unity. But because everyone is trying to discover their own purpose, pursuing their own "why," little gets accomplished. We trip over each other and complicate our efforts. However, when you have many people working toward the same purpose, you can accomplish much more.

If we all have one unified purpose, we can change the world.

What Will You Do Next?

The greatest misconception about love is that we naturally know how to do it well. But love is like everything else we want to be good at in life—we have to learn about it and practice it.

So what will you do next?

If you are committed to becoming a loving person, how will you grow?

Effective growth happens when it has clear direction and accountability. If you desire to continue your growth process you will need three key components:

- Community

- Process

- Time

Community

On day 10 we introduced you to a community of people called the Growth Junkies who are learning and growing every day into more loving people.

How do you become a Growth Junkie?

Begin by listening to the *Growth Junkies Podcast*. It is designed to connect a community of people unified around the same purpose of becoming loving people.

The podcast is built around a process that begins with our personal stories and how love ought to be a way of life. It is a great resource to help expedite your growth.

Process

As Growth Junkies, we believe a person becomes more loving by developing a healthy life emotionally, relationally, intellectually, and vocationally. During your journey through this book, you've already begun to dig into these areas of your life.

To take it a step further, we encourage you to begin working through our personal development experience called *The Four Dimensions of Human Health.* Many of the topics have been discussed on the podcast and it provides structure for the process of growth.

You can download a PDF for free on our website LoveandTransformation.org or you can purchase a printed copy on Amazon.

No matter how healthy you are, you can always grow in these areas.

If you're interested in learning more about the four dimensions, you can take an assessment at LoveandTransformation.org/Store.

Time

Change takes time.

Once you are surrounded by people who are unified around a process for growth, you're in a great position to see the change you desire. But executing the process over a long period of time is what will eventually produce the results you're looking for.

Time gives you the opportunity to experiment and test the process you've put in place. Unfortunately, people often give up right before they see a spike of growth. In an effort to avoid this, we suggest the following two steps:

First, share your intentions for growth with a couple of trusted friends who can encourage you along the way.

Second, evaluate your progress every three months. Keep track of the areas you are seeking to address and any changes that take place.

Just these two simple steps will help you to keep going and make the most of your time.

Experience Transformation by Trusting an Expert

"Any fool can know. The point is to understand."
—Albert Einstein

In our current information age, anyone can easily establish themselves as an expert by claiming to know something you don't. The value in Einstein's quote above is that anyone can "know" something but understanding means finding out if it really works.

Personal discovery of wisdom is a lost art in our modern way of thinking. It has been sacrificed to loud voices, flashy presentations, and crafty agendas.

Dictionary.com defines wisdom as "the knowledge of what is true and right coupled with just judgment as to action; discernment; insight."

If your car breaks down, do you take the advice of someone who knows nothing about cars, or do you take it to an expert?

Of course, you're going to take it to a mechanic.

We all need experts we can trust to lead us down the right path to success in whatever we're trying to achieve.

If you want to be a loving person, you should find an example who is an expert.

Who might that be?

Who's the expert on love? Where do we go for that?

We're not the experts on love, even though that's what this book is about.

If you want to find out who *we* think is the ultimate expert on love, keep reading.

Find an Expert

What questions would you ask the ultimate expert on love?

1.

2.

3.

Where would you go to find an expert on love, someone you could learn from?

What makes the source you identified qualified to be an expert on love?

"Love your neighbor as yourself."

—Jesus of Nazareth

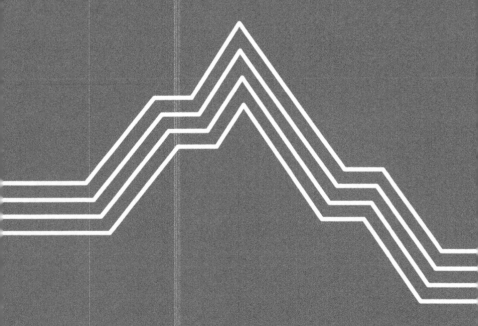

DAY 18

The Missing Chapter

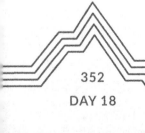

If the concepts in this book resonate with you and you want to go deeper, there's one more chapter that can help you take this to the next level.

Go to LoveandTransformation.org/MissingChapter to read the missing chapter.

(Don't worry, it's completely free—we won't ask for your email or anything.)

Let's Get More People Talking About Love

We cannot change culture alone. To tip the scales of power from fear to love, we must have a collaborative effort. We need your help. The tipping point is 10 percent—10 percent of people living a life of love will revolutionize our culture.

If you've been following along and completing the exercises throughout this book, you've already started living a life of love. You've already begun to cast out your fears. Reflect on the time you've spent with this book.

What has changed in your life?

What have you learned?

You don't have to agree with everything we've said. In fact, if you disagree, that's great—we're challenging you to think for yourself. But if you believe that more love would make the world a better place, then set an example. We're challenging you to make love the way you shape culture.

Make these concepts more than just a book you read. Make this part of your life. Inspire others to do the same.

If *MEGALIFE* has helped you, invite others to go through it as well. Find one other person to share the book with or start a group to go through the book one day at a time and engage in discussions. Support each other as you work together to create lives centered on love.

Join The Movement

The digital heart graphic below symbolizes the electrical current of love that binds us together. We have developed a special sticker that can be shipped to you. It has been designed for water bottles, laptops, and vehicles. If you would like to display your commitment to becoming a loving person, the sticker can be found our website.

Crossword Answer Key

1. Benevolence – Desire to do good to others; an act of kindness; a charitable gift

2. Friend – A person attached to another by feelings of affection or personal regard

3. Happiness – Characterized by or indicative of pleasure, contentment, or joy

4. Loyalty – Faithfulness to commitments or obligations

5. Desire – A longing or craving, as for something that brings satisfaction or enjoyment

6. Unity – Oneness of mind, feeling, etc., as among a number of persons

7. Passion – Any powerful or compelling emotion or feeling

8. Anxiety – Full of mental distress or uneasiness because of fear of danger or misfortune

9. Culture – The behaviors and beliefs characteristic of a particular group of people

10. Motive – Something that causes a person to act in a certain way, do a certain thing, etc.

11. Stress – Physical, mental, or emotional strain or tension

12. Worry – To torment oneself with or suffer from disturbing thoughts

13. Security – Freedom from danger, risk, care, anxiety, or doubt; well-founded confidence.

14. Joy – The emotion of great delight caused by something exceptionally good or satisfying; keen pleasure

15. Altruism – The principle or practice of unselfish concern for or devotion to the welfare of others

15. Admiration – A feeling of wonder, pleasure, or approval

16. Compromise – A settlement of differences by mutual concessions

17. Emotion – Any strong agitation of the feelings actuated by experiencing love, hate, fear, etc., and usually accompanied by certain physiological changes

18. Relationship – An emotional or other connection between people

19. Family – A group of people or things that are related by common characteristics, features, or properties

19. Fear - Anticipation of the possibility that something unpleasant will occur

20. Love – Strong predilection, enthusiasm, or liking for anything

21. Trust – Confident expectation of something

22. Hatred – Intense dislike; extreme aversion or hostility

ACKNOWLEDGMENTS

We want to thank Steve and Barbara Uhlmann, without whom the Love and Transformation Institute would not exist.

We also want to thank Roger and Casey Sloan, without whom this book would not have been written.

We also want to thank all of our partners, supporters, and clients without whom we could not produce our programs and resources.

Thanks to the team at Aloha Publishing, including Maryanna Young, Megan Terry, and Heather Geotter, for their help in developing this book.

And, last of all, we want to thank our families, without whose support we could not pursue our plans and dreams.

ABOUT THE AUTHORS

About LTI

Love and Transformation Institute (LTI) is a non-profit organization dedicated to leveraging the love of God to transform individuals and organizations by providing resources and creating experiences to inspire change and influence society. At LTI we believe that love is the chief catalyst for personal and cultural transformation. Toward this end, we develop resources and provide experiences that help people and teams put love into practice so that they can get healthy and grow.

Ben Bost

Ben is the co-founder of the Love & Transformation Institute and the operational leader and creative director. He has a background in digital technology, media, content curation, mentoring, and organizational leadership.

A former professional golfer, Ben transitioned his years on the golf course into mentoring world-class athletes and business leaders. From 2006-2016, Ben was the Senior Director for the Fellowship of Christian Athletes Golf Ministry. During this time, Ben served as Spring Training chaplain to the Los Angeles Angels of Anaheim through Baseball Chapel and the traveling community on the PGA Tour.

Ben holds a BA in history and religious studies (UCLA, Baylor University) and an MA in biblical leadership from Phoenix Seminary.

Ben lives in Eagle, Idaho, with his wife, Carrie, and three children: Joshua, Eli, and Audrey.

Dr. Kent Delhousaye

Kent is the co-founder of the Love & Transformation Institute and the visionary leader and primary communicator.

Before launching LTI, Kent was a pastor for 20 years at churches in California and Arizona. Kent is a certified executive coach, a published author, a songwriter, and a college and seminary professor. He authored the book *Blueprint in Bedlam* and co-wrote the worship album *Unexpected Blessing*. He has served as an adjunct professor at Grand Canyon University, Phoenix Seminary, and Ecola Bible College.

Kent has a BA in public relations from Arizona State University, a MDiv in biblical communication from Phoenix Seminary, a DMin in philosophical theology from the Talbot School of Theology at Biola University, and a graduate certificate in professional executive coaching from the Townsend Institute at Concordia University Irvine.

Kent and his wife, Stephanie, live in Eagle, Idaho, with their three children: Ethan, Christian, and Claire.

Made in the USA
Las Vegas, NV
01 July 2022